Twayne's United States Authors Series

EDITOR OF THIS VOLUME

Kenneth E. Eble

University Of Utah

Gene Stratton Porter

TUSAS 364

Gene Stratton Porter

GENE STRATTON PORTER

By BERTRAND F. RICHARDS

Emeritus, Indiana State University

TWAYNE PUBLISHERS
A DIVISION OF G. K. HALL & CO., BOSTON

Copyright © 1980 by G. K. Hall & Co.

Published in 1980 by Twayne Publishers,
A Division of G. K. Hall & Co.
All Rights Reserved

Printed on permanent/durable acid-free paper and bound
in the United States of America

First Printing

Library of Congress Cataloging in Publication Data

Richards, Bertrand F
Gene Stratton Porter.

(Twayne's United States authors series ; TUSAS 364)
Bibliography: p. 151-61
Includes index.
1.   Porter, Gene Stratton, 1863-1924—
Criticism and interpretation.
PS3531.07345Z77   818'.5'209   79-24477
ISBN 0-8057-7304-5

To Jane

Contents

About the Author

Bertrand Field Richards was born on April 18, 1910 in Newton, Illinois. His initial endeavor at higher education was terminatd by the depression of the thirties. After many experiences unrelated to education, including service in the Second World War, he resumed his formal schooling and made teaching his career. His educational background is as follows: Rice Institute (now University), 1929–31; University of Illinois and University of Michigan (ASTP), 1943; Eastern Illinois University (B.S., 1959); Indiana State University (M.A., 1961); and post-graduate work since the M.A. in English, semiotic, and psychology at Indiana State. He received his Ph.D with Phi Beta Kappa from Duke University in 1971.

Dr. Richards taught for seven years at Newton Community High School and for thirteen years at Indiana State University. He was actively engaged in research in semantics and composition. He was for ten years a member of the Board of Directors of the National Council of Teachers of English and a member of the National Committee on Semantics in the Secondary Schools. He has published in the field of his special interest and has also written articles of literary explication and criticism.

Since his retirement in 1976, he has devoted his time to independent writing. He has long been interested in nature and in gardening—his first publication was a garden article in Better Homes and Gardens in 1939. He now lives in Indianapolis with his wife, Jane.

Preface

This book makes no attempt to establish Gene Stratton Porter as a prominent figure in the literature of the United States. On the other hand it does not ignore the fact that her books sold and were read by millions of people in the early decades of this century. To dismiss as of no importance the approval of popular taste is to accuse the reading public of a lack of intelligence; while such a lack often seems apparent, still the phenomenon of acceptance remains which must be explained. That there are minor currents as well as major currents in American thought cannot be denied, and often the minor currents are important in themselves. This book does attempt to reach an understanding as to why Gene Stratton Porter's books appealed to so many people.

Gene Stratton Porter wrote twelve novels in the period between the publication of her first, *The Song of the Cardinal*, in 1903, and her twelfth, *The Keeper of the Bees*, which was written in the year before her death in 1924 but which was not published until the following year, 1925. From the point of sales, all of them were successful, and four were phenomenal. She early developed a formula for success and stuck with it throughout her writing career. But other writers also using a formula failed to achieve the same degree of success. This book will examine the formula, the literary themes, and the craftsmanship of the novels which made them the best-sellers that they were in the opening years of the century.

In spite of the eminently successful fiction that she wrote, if Gene Stratton Porter is to occupy any permanent place in the history of American letters, that place will no doubt be established by her work as a nature lover and a nature writer and photographer. Therefore, not only the nature books themselves but the nature content of the novels must be considered, and the question must be posed as to how much the illustration of her books contributed to their success.

Because of her popularity and because of her sales, Gene

Stratton Porter was able to demand of her publishers that she be allowed to alternate novels and books about nature. The sales of the former more than made up for any losses of the latter, which were by the bookmaking standards of her time very expensive projects indeed. Both the content and the influence of these nature books and the similarity between them and the natural history embodied in the novels will be examined.

The popularity, appeal, and worth of Gene Stratton Porter can best be understood by realizing that—at least for thousands of her readers—she was the right writer for her time. The change from an agrarian to an industrial and metropolitan society had almost been completed, but there remained a large portion of the country which was essentially rural. Her novels will be viewed as escapist for these people in that they helped ease the strain of a life which was rapidly becoming too mechanical.

There are some writers of whom it can be said that their lives are utterly divorced from their writings. There are others whose works are quite clearly influenced by their lives and times although their books are in no sense autobiographical. And then there are others—among them Gene Stratton Porter—in whom life and work are inseparable. Her nature books, being the stories of her own experiences as a photographer of nature, are of course stories of her life. The novels, being as was her intention nature stories with an overlay of fiction to make them palatable to the readers of popular magazines and books, also drew heavily from her experiences and reflect her life. Although only one of the novels, *Laddie,* is unashamedly autobiographical in that it depicts her own childhood, there is a certain amount of Gene Stratton Porter discernible in both major and minor characters throughout her books. Quite frequently she writes herself into her books in the character of the Bird Woman, but the contacts with and the reactions of various characters to nature are those of Gene Stratton Porter herself.

Therefore, Chapter 1 deals with the life of the author as it accounts for and relates to her work. It is in no sense intended as a complete biographical sketch. It is only meant to illustrate how the events and the activities of living were reflected in the fiction and in the nature studies she produced. It is a more or less chronological relating, since the events that shaped the career of the writer grew out of the sequence of happenings as they occurred from year to year.

Chapter 2 shows with even more exactitude how the events of Porter's life shaped the careers that grew out of that life. The various kinds of writing she did are presented and her remarkable activity as a photographer of nature and illustrator of her own books is discussed. In this chapter Porter's poetic output is discussed along with her desire to be remembered as a poet rather than as a novelist. Discussion of the poetry here seemed appropriate rather than the devotion of an entire chapter to her rather meager contribution to this field of endeavor. Other minor and miscellaneous writings are not neglected. That these careers united and culminated in her effort to produce "decent" faithful motion picture versions of her stories is not ignored.

Chapters 3 and 4 discuss Porter's literary output. Chapter 3 gives a brief synopsis of each of the novels and comments on them. Chapter 4 follows the same pattern with the nature books and with the miscellaneous works.

Chapter 5 deals with Porter's appropriateness for the time in which she lived and wrote. Her great popularity and her phenomenal sales records are probed. The chapter concludes with a discussion of the critical appraisal of her work and Porter's response to criticism.

Chapter 6 attempts to look at Porter from the perspective of the present day and to surmise as to what her position will be when more time has elapsed in the progression of the history of American culture.

As is natural for a work of this kind, the author incurred many debts in the preparation of this book, and particular expressions of gratitude are due to the following:

To James Leo Meehan, Jr., and John E. Meehan, grandsons of Gene Stratton Porter, and to Mrs. Anastasia Clothier Hathaway, a grandniece, who so graciously shared remembrances of Porter.

To Mrs. June Doggett of Rome City, Indiana, who provided much background material concerning Wildflower Woods; to Ms. Ruth Ann Figgins, secretary of the Gene Stratton-Porter Memorial Association, and to Mrs. Carolyn Sprunger, curator of the Gene Stratton Porter Memorial in Geneva, both of whom pointed to many sources of information.

To Mr. Rollin King of Muncie, Indiana, for much information, especially that concerning Miss Katharine Minahan and also concerning Porter's career as motion picture producer.

To Mr. David MacLean of Decatur, Indiana, whose Bibliography of Porter would have been even more helpful had it been published before the research for this book was almost completed.

Gratitude to the libraries in which work was done must be expressed. Especial thanks are due to Dr. Sul Lee, Dr. Robert O'Neill, and to Mr. Earl Tannenbaum of the Indiana State University Library who opened up their rare book room and made their extensive Porter collection available to the author. The materials on Gene Stratton Porter in the Indiana Room of the Indiana State Library were sources of valuable information, and the staff was most helpful. The Indianapolis Public Library, and the libraries of Indiana, Purdue, and Ball State Universities were sources of useful information. Much material was gleaned from the Library of Congress and from public libraries in New York, Chicago, and Denver.

Mr. Ken McCormick, Senior Consulting Editor of Doubleday and Company, Incorporated, the successors to Doubleday, Page and Company, was helpful in many ways, especially in the securing of permission to quote from Porter's writing. The author acknowledges, specifically, gratitude for the right to quote the letter from Christopher Morley to Mr. F. N. Doubleday, the selections from *The Firebird* and *Jesus of the Emerald,* and, generally, for permission to quote extensively from the writings of Gene Stratton Porter and Jeannette Porter Meehan.

Acknowledgment is due the Hearst Corporation for permission to reprint the poem "Blue Eyed Mary" from the May 1921 issue of *Good Housekeeping* and for the selection from *Euphorbia* from the January 1923 issue of the same magazine.

A word of explanation as to the use of the author's name is perhaps necessary. Because practically all modern indexes list the name as "Porter" rather than "Stratton-Porter" the hyphen has been eliminated in this volume except in quoted material. Gene Stratton Porter always referred to herself as "Mrs. Porter," although she used the hyphenated form on all her books and articles; however, the *Readers' Guide* during the years in which she was writing listed her under "Porter."

Finally, the author must express his thanks to his wife, Jane, for her forbearance and for the real help she has been to him in the preparation of the manuscript of this book.

BERTRAND F. RICHARDS

Indianapolis

Chronology

1863   Geneva Grace Stratton born August 17, at Hopewell Farm near LaGro in Wabash County, Indiana; daughter of Mark and Mary (Schallenberger) Stratton; youngest of twelve children, nine of whom were living at her birth.

1872   Brother, Leander (Laddie), drowned in Wabash River.

1874   Stratton family moved to Wabash because of illness of Mrs. Stratton; Geneva entered school.

1875   Death of Mary Stratton.

1881   First visit to Sylvan Lake at Rome City, Indiana.

1883   Death of sister, Anastasia Taylor; failed to finish high school; again visited Sylvan Lake; saw but did not meet her future husband, Charles Dorwin Porter.

1884   Began correspondence with Mr. Porter.

1886   Married Charles D. Porter; lived in Decatur, Indiana; name shortened to "Gene."

1888   Daughter Jeannette born.

1890   Porter family moved to Geneva, Indiana; death of Mark Stratton.

1893   Visited World's Fair in Chicago; gained ideas for home to be built in Geneva (Limberlost Cabin).

1895   Limberlost Cabin completed and occupied; received first camera as a Christmas gift from Jeannette.

1900   First publication in *Recreation;* beginning of series of "Camera Notes" bylined "Gene S. Porter" extending to May 1901.

1901   Publication in *Outing* in February; intermittent publication until September 1902; first fiction, "Laddie, the Princess, and the Pie," published in *Metropolitan*, September 1901; continued writing for *Metropolitan* until November 1903.

1903   *The Song of the Cardinal,* her first book, published by Indianapolis firm of Bobbs-Merrill in May.

1904   *Freckles* published; first book issued by Doubleday, Page & Company.

1905   Commissioned by Edward W. Bok to write series of bird articles illustrated with her own photographs for *Ladies' Home Journal.*

1906   *What I Have Done with Birds,* the *Journal* series, published April through August.

1907   *What I Have Done with Birds* published in book form by Bobbs-Merrill and *At the Foot of the Rainbow* issued by the Outing Company, New York.

1909   *A Girl of the Limberlost* published by Doubleday; *Birds of the Bible* published by Jennings and Graham, Cincinnati, Ohio; Jeannette married and moved to Buffalo, New York; Lorene Miller (later, Mrs. Frank N. Wallace) employed as secretary.

1910   Acquired land and began plans for new home and sanctuary at Sylvan Lake; *Music of the Wild* published by Jennings and Graham.

1911   *After the Flood* by Bobbs-Merrill; *The Harvester* by Doubleday, Page & Company, who from then on were to be her exclusive publishers.

1912   *Moths of the Limberlost;* building Limberlost Cabin North.

1913   *Laddie;* death of brother, Lemon (Leon of *Laddie*); daughter, Leah Mary, left in Gene Stratton Porter's care.

1914   Limberlost Cabin North completed and moved into in spring.

1915   *Michael O'Halloran.*

1916   *Morning Face.*

1917   *What I Have Done with Birds* reissued as *Friends in Feathers.*

1918   *A Daughter of the Land.*

1919   Made first trip to California in October.

1920   Decided to make California her permanent home.

1921   *Her Father's Daughter;* Harry B. Burton, editor of *McCall's,* came to California and requested that she do a series of editorials for him. First appearance of "Gene Stratton-Porter's Page" in December.

1922   *The Fire Bird;* formed company to produce her own films; Jeannette married James Leo Meehan, Mrs. Porter's director.

1923   *The White Flag* serialized in *Good Housekeeping;* pub-

lished as book in August; *Wings* and *Jesus of the Emerald;*
Euphorbia serialized in *Good Housekeeping.*

1924   Building California homes on Catalina Island and in the
Bel Air section of Los Angeles; serialization of *Tales You
Won't Believe* in *Good Housekeeping;* death of sister,
Katherine Marshall; in November left Catalina to spend
winter in Los Angeles; died as a result of a collision
between her limousine and a street car on December 6;
interment in mausoleum in Hollywood Memorial Park.

1925   *Tales You Won't Believe* issued in book form; *The Keeper
of the Bees* published after serialization in *McCall's;*
release of the motion picture version at the same time.

1927   *The Magic Garden* published after serialization in
McCall's, and *Let Us Highly Resolve,* a gathering from the
editorial pages contributed to the same magazine.

CHAPTER 1

The Life That Touched
Fifty Million Lives

I *The Beginnings*

IT is not often that the life and works of an author are so
intermingled that it is impossible to consider one as separated
from the other. But such is the case with Gene Stratton Porter.
Her life was her work, and her work was drawn from her life
itself. By her own admission, everything that she wrote was
taken from her own life and experience, and changed, modified,
and manipulated as might be to suit her needs; but there was still
only one source for her—her memories.

What, then, was this life from which all of Gene Stratton
Porter's literary and artistic work grew!

Pity the biographer who attempts a definitive life of Gene
Stratton Porter. Grant Overton states concerning her: "Her
autobiography written in 1914 has never been published in
full."[1] So far as can be determined, this autobiography (if it ever
did exist) has still never been published. All the evidence seems
to point that Overton's "autobiography" may have been the
material prepared for *Chambers Journal* (London) which was
indeed published. This account seems to contain what Gene
Stratton Porter wished her readers to know of her life.[2] "My Life
and My Books," which appeared in the *Ladies' Home Journal* in
1916, rewrites the *Chambers* material and presents it to the
American public.[3] These few pages would be all the biographer
could draw from which was authentic Porter were it not for
statements made in the magazine articles she published and in
her books. In 1915, in response to public demand, her publishers
brought out an account of her life written by Eugene Francis
Saxton and based in part on the English publication.[4] The Saxton

17

pamphlet was reprinted in H. E. Maule's volume concerning the Country Life Press in 1919.[5]

But for most investigators there is one main source for information concerning Gene Stratton Porter, *A Lady of the Limberlost: The Life and Letters of Gene Stratton-Porter,* by her daughter, Jeannette Porter Meehan. While Mrs. Porter was almost secretive in her efforts to insure her own privacy, and while there seems a decided tendency on her part to control what the public was to know of her, it seems almost certain that had she lived, her autobiography would have been one of her prime projects. It also seems likely that those biographical materials which were at hand after her death were utilized in the account written by her daughter.

The Meehan book was put together shortly after Porter's death. It consists of the daughter's remembrances of her mother, the autobiographical notes referred to, letters to and from Porter, and excerpts from articles published in magazines. Unfortunately, few of these items are clearly identified. This fact need not deter the casual reader, but it makes any scholarly investigation difficult. Often the names of senders or receivers of letters are omitted, and the absence of dates leads to many perplexities—even to disbelief.

One example is sufficient: on page 359 of the Meehan book, the first line has Mr. Porter "twenty years older than Mother," and the bottom of the same page has him dying "almost exactly two years after Mother's accident" at the age of seventy-six. Gene Stratton Porter was sixty-one at the time of her death, which would have made Mr. Porter seventy-four and the age difference only thirteen years. But another source reduces the gap to eight years.[6] According to the date of Charles Dorwin Porter's birth as given in the vital statistics for Adams County, Indiana, as April 3, 1851, the actual difference was twelve years and four months.[7]

Almost all writers of biographical sketches of Porter refer to her husband as Charles Darwin Porter. Meehan is specific that the name is Dorwin; there were cousins named Dorwin. The change most likely came about because of association with Charles Darwin, the evolutionist. Mrs. Bailey even gives the name a decided Gallic flavor by spelling it "D'Arwin."[8] Such matters are, of course, inconsequential; they only illustrate the difficulties the researcher encounters in investigating the life of the author.

Just as the life of Gene Stratton Porter cannot be separated from her work, neither can it be separated from her land. Her land, her actual vicinity, was a part of almost everything she wrote. This is true of the Indiana novels, but it is true of the California books as well. There is, however, this difference. The Indiana landscape was that into which she was born and in which she matured; the California landscape was acquired and interpreted in the terms of the familiar homeland. What then was this land which produced and nurtured Gene Stratton Porter?

Before settlement began, there stretched from Grand Lake St. Mary's in Ohio to the glaciated shore of Lake Michigan a vast area of forest, lakes, and swamps. This was a high region formed by the ancient upheaval of the Cincinnati Arch and draining variously into the Great Lakes–St. Lawrence system and into the Ohio River basin. The St. Mary's and the Wabash Rivers are only fourteen miles apart at Decatur, Indiana.

But by the time Geneva Grace Stratton was born during the Civil War year of 1863, the Wabash valley area near LaGro where the Stratton family lived had been settled, its forests cleared, and farmsteads established. It was land removed only a step from the wilderness. On the prairies to the west, buffalo still abounded. The rivers and streams were filled with fish. Birds were everywhere. The great flocks of passenger pigeons still flew over Indiana. Wild turkeys, prairie chicken, and quail were hunted for the table. Deer and bear were plentiful, as were smaller game animals. The streams and lakes abounded with fish. Geneva remembered the clearing of much forest land and tells of the great fires from the burning of what would become priceless timber but which was then a commodity of no use. The seeds of conservancy were sown here. In *Tales You Won't Believe* she writes, "In pain, confusion and futile protest I watched the buffalo disappear from the prairies; the red horse, the bass, and the wood ducks from the forest; while as exquisite wild flowers as the circle of the globe knew vanished from the face of the earth" (p. 163).

The Indian uprisings were over although there remained Indian families interspersed with the settlers. She writes that all my life I have been steeped in Indian tradition and history, having been born and reared near the camping ground of the Potawotamies and the Miamis, and in my childhood I frequently visited the home of Chief Wacacoonah. My father and mother married and began life among the Indians. When I lived in Wabash, Indiana, I was bounded on the west by the Miami Reservation, who boasted descendants of Logan, although his immediate family was supposed to have been wiped out. John Logan, however, claimed a rather immediate relationship with the old chief of the Mingoes. On the south we had old Chief Wacacoonah of the Meshingmesas and hundreds of his tribe among whom I circulated freely as a child, being well acquainted with the old chief's daughters, Nancy and Susan, and of having been entertained in the old chief's home with my brother-in-law, who was an Indian agent and the guardian for many members of these tribes.[9]

Mark and Mary Stratton had come to this area from Ohio, had established their homestead, and had eleven children when Geneva arrived. Two sisters, Samaria and Louisa, her immediate elders, had died of whooping cough or scarlet fever or a combination of the two, leaving an age separation of nine years between Geneva and her next older sister, Ada. Her elder brothers and sisters, Katherine, Anastasia, Jerome, Mary Ann, and Irvin, were either married or away from home at school or on business. The family left at home consisted of Father and Mother Stratton, Florence, Leander, Lemon, Ada, and Geneva Grace.

Mary Stratton, a "little Dutch woman with a gift for growing things," had never fully recovered from the same illness which had afflicted her daughters. She was a semi-invalid during all of Geneva's early girlhood. This fact led to Geneva's being "raised" more or less by her father and brothers. She spent more time out of doors with them than indoors with her mother and sisters, and she became familiar with nature as it existed all around her. A sensitive child, she responded to the stimuli of the outdoors and developed an abiding interest in the creatures and plants that surrounded her. Her first lessons in ecology and conservation came from her father, who impressed upon her the importance of the balance of nature, and from her mother, who taught her plant lore and the necessity for transplanting to her own wildflower garden only those plants which were threatened with extinction elsewhere.

Geneva was particularly interested in the birds, especially with nests and nestlings, and learned to overcome the natural fears inspired in birds by humans to the extent that she was able to feed the young in their nests. A playful "gift" from her father, which she took quite seriously, of all the birds on their farm (and in all the universe) only intensified her interest.[10] These occupations of her earliest childhood influenced all the writing of Gene Stratton Porter. There were other interests, of course, but they were to come later. The detailing of this early life appears in the novel *Laddie,* which recounts the story of her early years. In this book she is Little Sister and Leander, her brother, is Laddie.

Leander was the oldest brother at home, and he devoted much time to the upbringing of Geneva, taking her to the fields with him and watching over her play and observations of nature. Her father was the most influential person in her life—as she admits—but Leander was almost equally important to her childhood.[11] It was Leander's intention to remain on the farm and succeed his father in its ownership. But just before his nineteenth birthday, Leander drowned in the Wabash River.

This blow to the family further weakened Mary Stratton's health, and the loss of a successor to the farmland so destroyed Mark Stratton's hopes that life in the country was no longer feasible. The Strattons moved to Wabash, the closest town, which had some 2,500 people, and where an older sister, Anastasia Taylor, lived. This removal to the county seat meant a doctor at close proximity for Mary Stratton and school for Geneva.

The young wildling was not fond of school, but because of the insistence and influence of her father she remained enrolled and became a fairly apt pupil. Even this early in her life, the desire— even the necessity—to succeed at whatever she attempted was firmly entrenched.

Mrs. Stratton lived only four months after the family moved to Wabash. Following her death, Mark Stratton and his brood, consisting of Irvin (who was unmarried and connected with the Wabash schools), Florence, Ada, Lemon, and Geneva, continued to live with the Taylors. Geneva progressed in school but shortened her name to Geneve.

Not much can be said for Geneve Stratton's education in the

public schools other than that it was the usual for that time. Her real education was self-education, and it came mostly from her reading and from the tutelage of her father. She never finished high school. During her last year she dropped out to care for her sister, Anastasia Taylor, and after Mrs. Taylor's death she never returned. She seems to have had little regret for this lack of a formal education until later in her life. She continued to read and to study and to acquire the education that really mattered to her—that which she could attain through her own efforts and under the guidance of her father. Mark Stratton himself was self-educated; he read widely in history and in the Bible, and he seems to have had an incredible memory. The books he had were not many, but they were thoroughly used.

Among the authors specifically named by Porter which give evidence of her reading at this period of her life are George Eliot, Bulwer, Hugo, Dumas, and Jane Porter. She mentions reading *Romola* and *Scottish Chiefs*. It is curious that there is no reference to Shakespeare, to the poets, or to the Bible; but, of course, that would be a book for study, not for reading for pleasure or secular education. As a young matron in Geneva, Indiana, she prepared a paper for a ladies' literary club in which she cites Tennyson, Emerson, Thoreau, Ruskin, Dr. Johnston, D. G. Rossetti, and Matthew Arnold. Evidently the number of books available to her had increased somewhat. Much later in her life, it is evident that she knew the work of the great naturalists—Fabre, Muir, Thompson, Mills, and John Burroughs. She greatly admired the works of Burroughs and avidly read him, although he refused to read her.[12]

Gene Stratton Porter left no catalog of her reading; however, there are references in articles and letters. Longfellow and Christina Rossetti became favorites, but, surprisingly, so did George Bernard Shaw. In a letter to a critic she adds Washington Irving, Whittier, Joaquin Miller, and Confucius to her list.[13] These authors are only a sampling of those she must have read in the course of her self-education, which was lifelong.

She educated herself in other fields, too. She studied music—banjo, piano, and violin—and painting—both watercolor and oil. In the article mentioned, "What My Father Meant to Me," Mrs. Porter tells that the Stratton family was not rich. She states that she was more poorly dressed than her classmates and that her father exchanged produce—butter and eggs, fruits and vegetables—which he brought in from his farm for her painting lessons.

In regard to her clothing, Mrs. Porter, writing for *McCall's* late in her life, referred to this circumstance:

Among girls I know, from bitter personal experience, what happens to the daughter of a Methodist minister who has not the fancy ribbons, the silk and velvet school dresses, the high-heeled shoes. I will say for myself that I weathered the storm, but with bitter heartburnings, and got all the education coming my way. And I will further add that in after life when I have had the money to dress as I chose, I still have tried to make the garments I wore exactly suited to the occasion and the place in which I appeared in them.[14]

The double shame of being poorly dressed and of having to pay for in produce for what other girls were paying for in cash made a lasting imprint on the character of Gene Stratton Porter which is reflected in many of the novels. It seems evident that in writing of Elnora Comstock's tribulations as a beginning high school student in *A Girl of the Limberlost* Porter was mirroring her own experiences in entering the school in Wabash.

II *Courtship and Marriage*

In the 1880s Sylvan Lake at Rome City, Indiana, was one of the most popular resorts in Indiana. In 1881 Geneve Stratton made her first visit to this lake. She and her sister Ada, were there to chaperone the courtship between their older sister Florence and Will Compton, the man Florence was later to marry. Geneve was entranced by the lake and welcomed the opportunity to visit it again the next summer.

On this second trip, she did not meet but *saw* her husband-to-be, Charles Dorwin Porter. A druggist from Geneva, Indiana, he was visiting the lake, saw Geneve and her group, was attracted to her, and had the temerity to write her, asking that they begin a correspondence. Geneve's response shows that she at this early stage in her life was the unconventional and strong-willed woman she was later so obviously to become. To correspond with a man to whom she had not even been introduced and whose letter indicated that his intent was more than mere friendship went against all the prohibitions of society. But Geneve did not care. She had also seen him and found him attractive, her life was her own, and she would do as she so pleased. She replied to Mr. Porter:

If you ever even *glanced* at me, I was totally *unconscious* of the fact, and had you not mentioned being on the train, I should not have remembered you. But if you noted me sufficiently to remember me this long, then I am sure that you saw also that I behaved in a quiet and ladylike manner. But can I keep it if I correspond with an entire stranger?

I cannot exactly see any harm, but won't you please not ask me to write again unless you are *certain* you can respect me as *much* as if you had formed my acquaintance in the authorized way.[15]

This letter also contains a curiosity in that it has in it the sentence, "I have three sisters and a brother who is all that's good and one who is all that's bad." Geneve Stratton at this time had three brothers, Jerome, Irvin, and Lemon. Nowhere else does she speak of a strained relationship with any one of them. Perhaps she was referring in jest to the ebullient and teasing Lemon, so faithfully depicted as Leon in *Laddie*.

So began a long series of letters. In the summer of 1885, after a full year's exchange, the couple finally met, again at Rome City. The correspondence continued, interspersed with visits, and culminated in marriage on April 21, 1886.

There are many and varying accounts of the shortening of "Geneve" to "Gene." There is one apocryphal story that it was because a tormenter in Geneva referred to her as "Geneva from Geneva," which sorely hurt the "shy and introverted Mrs. Porter."[16] But Gene Stratton Porter was neither shy nor introverted, and the shortening to "Geneve" had occurred long before the arrival in Geneva, Indiana. More persuasive evidence attributes the name change to her high-school days and to the name curtailment so common to youth. It is quite possible that this circumstance is true and that "Gene" became a nickname for "Geneva" or "Geneve." But the real evidence comes from the letters. Mr. Porter's first was addressed to Miss Genevieve Stratton. Her early letters to him are signed "Geneve," but the signature later became "Gene" or even "Genie." The calling card enclosed with the wedding invitations of 1886 bears the name "Gene Stratton."[17] It is apparent, then, that the change was firmly fixed in her mind during the courtship. However, Mark Stratton called her Geneva till his dying day.[18]

Although Mr. Porter's business was in Geneva, he considered it a village too small and uncouth for the establishment of his home, and the couple lived in Decatur, several miles to the north, which was much larger and which was the county seat. Mr. Porter commuted between Geneva and Decatur, using the "two a day, each way" passenger system of the Grand Rapids and Indiana Railroad. Decatur was, of course, much closer to the branch drugstore and banking interests which he had in Fort Wayne.

The commuting arrangement seems to have been rather haphazard and resulted for the most part in Mr. Porter's usually remaining in Geneva for the week and coming home only on weekends. There was a daily correspondence between him and his wife. Mrs. Porter busied herself with housekeeping, making a garden, becoming acquainted with the Porter family, and preparing for the birth of a baby.

III   *The Limberlost*

Gene Stratton Porter's first and only child, Jeannette, was born in Decatur in 1888. Shortly thereafter, in 1890, Mr. Porter, having decided that Geneva had improved as a place to live, and no doubt tired of the commuting arrangement, moved his family to Geneva. It was here that the second and perhaps the most important part of the life that made the writer unfolded. To the south and east of Geneva stretched the vastness of the great Limberlost Swamp, an area of bogs, streams, and virgin forest which was to serve as a laboratory for her studies of natural history and which provided the setting for many of her novels and books of natural history.

There is a mistaken notion about Gene Stratton Porter that she was born and reared in the Limberlost swamp region that she made famous in her novels and nature books. The fact is that she had no real acquaintance with the swamps of Northeast Central Indiana until after her marriage and her removal to Geneva, which lay on the borders of the Limberlost. She was born and her girlhood was spent in the gently rolling basin of the Wabash River in Wabash County. The land had long been cleared of its original forest and consisted mainly of farms with the usual makeup of homesteads, tilled fields, pastures, orchards, and woodlots.

Gene Stratton Porter was, therefore, not of the Limberlost born and bred. Most writers and critics assume that her upbringing was that of Elnora Comstock in *A Girl of the Limberlost*—that she had known the swamp from earliest childhood. Such is not the truth. Gene Stratton Porter was unacquainted with the swamp until after her marriage. Even the brief sojourn in Decatur was somewhat remote from the swamp, and it was not until she and her family moved to Geneva that she became aware of and intimate with the Limberlost. None of the sources for the life of Gene Stratton Porter gives a clear account of her introduction to the swamp. One writer described it thus:

In the course of her work Mrs. Porter had spent every other day for three months in the Limberlost Swamp, making a series of studies of the nest of a black vulture. Early in her married life she had met a Scotch lumberman, who told her of the swamp and of securing fine timber there for Canadian shipbuilders, and later when she had moved to within less than a mile of its northern boundary she met a man who was buying curly maple, black walnut, golden oak, wild cherry, and other wood extremely valuable for a big furniture factory in Grand Rapids. There was one particular woman, of all those the author worked among, who exercised herself most concerning her. (It was this woman's husband who drove the stake and ploughed around the kildeer's nest in the cornfield to save it for the author; and he did many other acts of kindness without understanding exactly what he was doing or why.)[19]

This woman became the Sarah Duncan of *Freckles*, and other characters in the book were drawn from people she knew in the area. A letter written by a friend of the Geneva days, Margaret Day Briggs, and printed in the Geneva Centennial Booklet in 1972 lists the origin of some of the other characters in Freckles: "Her people. . . , it may be of interest to know, are mostly local people. The Angel is her daughter Jeanette; The Man of Affairs, her husband; Freckles, Robert Black; and the Cook, William Wiley; the lumberman was a man by the name used in the book. All of our town."

Because of her late-coming to the region, one can only assume that Freckles's discovery of the Limberlost as a place of danger and terror is much more accurate for Porter than to assume that Elnora's lifelong knowledge of the swamp as a familiar place—to be respected for its dangers, but not to be feared—is that of the author.

The most accurate picture of the girlhood of Gene Stratton Porter is to be found in *Laddie* rather than in *Freckles* or *A Girl of the Limberlost,* for the setting of *Laddie* is that of her childhood home.

When the Porters moved to Geneva, they occupied a small house on a large lot complete with garden, orchard, a chicken-park, and a convenient yard for Jeannette to play in. There was a barn behind the house where the horse and buggy (sometimes a spring-wagon) which feature so prominently in accounts of Gene Stratton Porter's field work were kept.

It seems likely that Gene Stratton Porter's great and abiding interest in birds provided the stimulus that led her into the swamp. There were, of course, birds of all kinds over the Indiana of that day, but the closer one came to the swamp, the more plentiful they were and the deeper one penetrated, the greater the profusion. Appreciative as she was of the beauties of the swamp she could best express such beauty by a comparison with the birds.

Flashing through the treetops of the Limberlost there are birds whose colour is more brilliant than that of the gaudiest flower lifting its face to the sunlight. The lilies of the mire are not so white as the white herons that fish among them. The ripest spray of golden-rod is not so highly coloured as the burnished gold on the breast of the oriole that rocks on it. The jays are bluer than the calamus bed they wrangle above with throaty chatter. The finches are a finer purple than the ironwort; while for every clump of fox-fire flaming in the Limberlost there is a cardinal glowing redder on the bush above it.[20]

The record indicates that Gene Stratton Porter, strong willed and purposeful, was restless, The duties of wife, mother, and housekeeper were not onerous enough to stifle her need for self-expression. She maintained her interests in music and painting, but she most certainly doubted her talent to succeed along these lines to the recognition she so craved. For, though perhaps subconsciously, this was the force that drove Gene Stratton Porter—the desire to be somebody, to have her talents known and appreciated.

It seems that the idea of becoming a professional writer was instilled within Gene Stratton Porter quite early in her life. Undeniably, writing rather than photography was her first

intent. By her own account, she had written from earliest
childhood, and she speaks with regret of having destroyed a
great deal of her early work:

I cannot remember the time when I was not interested in poetry and
trying to write it, but I had some very discouraging advice when I was a
youngster, on the strength of which I burned three books of poetry, one
of which I would almost give my right arm to repossess today. . . . All
my life I have been writing things . . . and hiding them away because I
was too timid to let anyone see them. But . . . I wish to heaven I had
back again the material which I burned years ago. There is something
about the stuff that springs from the first young urge of the heart and
that is wet with the dew of youth and warmed with its enthusiasm that
does not come with such spontaneity after years of contact with the
world as it is met by most of us.[21]

She rather suggests that her motivation to succeed in her work
was primarily for money so that she could have material things.
There seems evident the drive of a strong-willed woman to
prepare herself for a fuller life than that of a rural Indiana
housewife.

In a "family" letter (not in Meehan but reported by her
grandniece, Anastasia Clothier Hathaway) written in 1890,
shortly after the move to Geneva, Mrs. Porter suggests that the
determination to become an author was firmly entrenched by
this time. She writes that "All my spare time is put in on the
Bible, Shakespeare and the Dictionary. . . . It's wonderful how
many people quote Shakespeare and don't know it or at least
from what play. I myself had forgotten that it was Cassio who
first bewailed his lost reputation. I don't believe there is a book
in the world so full of beautiful things as the Bible." And, most
importantly, she adds, "Someday I will tell you what my ambition
is and of the years of steady work which I have gone through
only in hope, not assurance of success," and "I have to pay dearly
for some of my wasted school days now."

It is impossible to know how much writing Porter was doing at
this time. By her own account in later years, she was constantly
writing and submitting to her father, poems, essays, and other
pieces for his criticism or approval. The rapidity of her
publication once she got started would certainly not rule out the
possibility of a closetful of manuscripts. Without doubt, she was

writing seriously and regularly long before her first article was published in 1900.

But the event which started Gene Stratton Porter on her career was insignificant enough in itself. It was the gift of a small camera which she received from her daughter at Christmas in 1895. She quickly mastered the use of this instrument and progressed to more advanced photography. She had found her medium. At one time she could tell the stories she knew of birds and nature, and she could illustrate these stories with pictures that would convince the most doubting of readers.

IV   *The Approaches to Fame—Head-shaking and Raised Eyebrows*

Gene Stratton Porter might never have penetrated the Limberlost and learned its secrets had progress not come to the area around Geneva. The Limberlost as pristine swampland was dangerous for anyone—let alone a woman—to venture far into its fastness. The name itself evolved from a young man named Jim Corbus but nicknamed "Limber" because of his tallness and leanness having been lost in the great Loblolly swamp, arousing so much hue and cry of "Limber's lost" that the name stuck to the region. But two events combined to make Porter's fieldwork possible and to bring about the destruction of the swamp. One was the discovery of the very valuable trees—wild cherry, golden oak, black walnut, and hard maple which it contained and which were being increasingly sought after by the furniture factories.

The other event was the discovery of profitable deposits of oil underlying the region. These discoveries opened up roads into the swamp, and brought men into it—men who were tolerant of and often helpful to this strange, fearless woman so intent on her own work.

The increased prosperity of the area was shared by the Porters. Mr. Porter organized a bank, expanded his drugstore, added a hotel to his interests, and bought a 365-acre farm. Shortly after the purchase of the farm the oil boom began, and the Porters profited from some sixty well-paying oil wells. Now mildly prosperous, they decided on a new house. They had visited the World's Fair in Chicago in 1893 and had been much impressed by the modern architecture displayed there. Utilizing some ideas she had gathered from visiting the Foresters' Building at the exposition, Mrs. Porter designed and had built a fourteen-room "cabin" of Wisconsin cedar logs and redwood which they named Limberlost Cabin. The house was completed and moved into in 1895.[22]

That Porter became more beloved by her readers than by her associates in her community is apparent. This was a rather natural occurrence because she imposed on herself such a schedule that she had little time for social amenities. In addition, she was highly unconventional in a day when unconventionality gave rise to suspicion. She dared to be different from the other women, and to so differ aroused intolerance and distrust. Yet she claims—and there seems no reason to doubt her—that her first duty was to keep a perfect household; to keep her rooms spotless, to prepare palatable and nutritious meals, and to make most of her daughter's dresses.[23] Only then would she allow herself time for fieldwork, for exploration of the Limberlost, and for writing.

Her longtime secretary, Lorene Miller Wallace, writing after Mrs. Porter's death, described the vigorous schedule imposed on the author by herself. Summers were devoted to field work, winters to writing, although not exclusively; some writing was done year round, and much observation was done in winter. When work was in progress, each morning was devoted to writing and no alterations of the schedule were allowed. The only intrusions permitted were when someone brought a wounded bird, a cocoon or moth, or a rare flower. Nature could intrude because nature was the material for the writing. There was a hiatus for lunch and a rest period. Afternoons were spent variously in field work, study, or revision. It was only when the day's work was completed that Porter allowed herself time for relaxation or social activity.[24]

Such a schedule obviously permitted little time for neighborliness or for socializing. Still, she did engage in church work, and she did belong to at least one woman's club, the Ladies' Literary Society of Geneva, for which she prepared and delivered a paper on Walt Whitman.[25] And there are also recorded instances of her entertaining friends at Limberlost Cabin. Marking her difference from the community was the fact that her entertainments were evening affairs, while the other women of the town would have afternoon social events. Mrs. Porter claimed that the summer afternoons were too hot; actually, she was unwilling to give up the time spent afield in her work with the natural history of the Limberlost. The letter from Mrs. Briggs describing her friend Mrs. Porter, relates some of the entertainments at Limberlost Cabin. She tells of music, card playing, and refreshments and calls her a charming hostess.

But the charming hostess was not the woman of the outdoors. "For her field work she used a knee-length khaki skirt with high leather hiking boots, a blouse or sweater of either brown or green, which blended with the outdoor colours, and a hat to match. She carried a revolver for protection."[26] A woman who dressed (as she often did) in boots and breeches and other various items of "man's" clothing, who went solitary and armed into territory where men seldom went alone, and who was doing something which was not by any stretch of the imagination "woman's work" was bound to be at least mildly alarming to her community.

The attitudes of the women of Geneva toward Mrs. Porter were in great part founded in jealousy and envy. Jealousy, perhaps, of the affluence which permitted such conduct, for the Porters were never poor—Limberlost Cabin was by far the largest house in the town—and envy of the spirit of the woman who dared pursue her own goal in the face of convention.

At any rate, Gene Stratton Porter was a woman chock full of energy and with the strength to sustain her ambition which was at this time to learn all that she could about nature—particularly about the photographing of birds in their natural surroundings—and to turn this knowledge into successful and profitable writing. To do so, she had to establish and adhere to a strict budgeting of her time which allowed little leeway for the social graces of the small-town woman's life.

But if Mrs. Porter was not overly popular with the women-folk of Geneva, she was well liked and readily accepted by the men who worked the Limberlost, the lumbermen, the oil workers, and the farmers. And she formed firm friendships with many of the farm women with whom she stopped for creature comforts and who hungered for companionship. Because of her real interest in people, she formed these friendships readily and sincerely. The fact that many of these men and women appear as characters in the novels does not suggest that she cultivated or studied these people with any ulterior purpose. But it is undeniable that these "rural" characters are among the most sympathetically and authentically drawn within the novels.

The record is by no means clear, but it is apparent that shortly after the Limberlost Cabin was built there were servants. At first a cook is mentioned, and a little later she begins to speak of a staff. Never well enumerated, there were in addition to household help always a secretary or two and a driver. Meehan mentions a picture taken in 1917 showing "the English house-keeper, the enormous Negro cook, and her inexperienced chauffeur, a lad of seventeen. . . ."[27]

While the account of Mrs. Porter going about her field work alone with her little black horse and her buggy or with her spring-wagon is explicit, it is not clear when she acquired her first automobile. Automobiles were becoming common, and Mrs. Porter was not reluctant to replace the horse-drawn vehicle with the horseless carriage. The motor car accepted without protest the interminable periods of waiting demanded by her field work. There is never any mention of her having learned to drive an automobile. One of her bitterest complaints against the privations of the First World War was that her driver was called into service.

V   First Publication

It has been impossible to determine how Gene Stratton Porter managed to get her first work published. Whether there were countless submissions and rejections or whether she met with instant success has not been revealed. The earliest publication discovered was in *Recreation* for February 1900. This issue contained an article by Porter and also the first of a series of columns on photography entitled "Camera Notes" bylined as by Gene S. Porter. The article, "A New Experience in Millinery," is indeed interesting in that it has a strong conservation intent; it deplores the slaughter of birds for their plumage to be used to decorate women's hats and urges the cessation of this practice. It suggests other and more suitable decoration, for example, ostrich plumes or peacock feathers, which can be taken without damaging the birds.

From February 1900 to May 1901, Gene Stratton Porter published three articles and seven columns in *Recreation*. Then, as Meehan puts it, "having had a little disagreement with the editor, she was given a place in the Natural History Department of *Outing*."[28] *Outing* was, as its name implies, a magazine devoted to all activities connected with the outdoors—sports, boating, camping, exploration, nature study, and conservation. It was her ability with the camera as well as with words that won her a place in the pages of this magazine, which was edited by Caspar Whitney.

The *Outing* articles extending from July 1901 to September 1902 were natural history with photographic offerings, the direct result of Porter's work in the Limberlost. There is no evidence from the magazine itself to indicate that she functioned in any editorial capacity in the "Natural History Department" of *Outing*.

In September 1901 Gene Stratton Porter's first fiction, "Laddie, the Princess, and the Pie," was published. It had been submitted to Perriton Maxwell, editor of *Metropolitan Magazine*. The return address had been lost, and the story published without the author's knowledge. This story was quickly followed in December 1901 by "How Laddie and the Princess Spelled Down at the Christmas Bee."

These early publications illustrate the two influences of the Limberlost and of her girlhood at work. The *Recreation* and *Outing* articles are pure Limberlost; the *Metropolitan* stories are pure girlhood. Two later Metropolitan story-articles are Limberlost. One can hardly doubt that the "Laddie" stories were ready and waiting, especially when one considers that the second story was commissioned, prepared, illustrated with her own photographs, and published in the short interval of September-December. She says that she had only a day and a half in which to do this work.[29]

By now Gene Stratton Porter was a professional writer, photographer, and illustrator with a wide following. And at about this time she made her first public appearance. She was invited to lecture at a Chautauqua in Coldwater, Michigan, where she was visiting a sister, Florence Compton. The "Bird Woman" had been featured in two of the *Metropolitan* stories and was obviously the author herself. When it was known that the Bird Woman was in town, the people demanded that she appear on one of the programs.[30] She had yet to publish her first book. But in 1903 *The Song of the Cardinal* appeared, and the career that grew out of a life was underway. It is known that she carried the manuscript to the offices of Bobbs-Merrill in Indianapolis herself. "I was so green that I did not know that a publishing house had an editor, so I asked for the secretary."[31] Matters were soon straightened out, however, and she not only saw the editor but emerged with a contract for the publication of her book.

VI *Writer and Conservationist*

The Porters remained in Geneva until 1913. By that time the destruction of the Limberlost—through lumbering, oil development, drainage, and cultivation—had almost been accomplished, and the laboratory for Gene Stratton Porter's field work was no longer productive. But the area around Sylvan Lake had not as yet suffered such devastation. As early as 1910, Mrs. Porter began considering a move to the area and by 1911 the project was under way. With six successful novels and four nature books behind her, Gene Stratton Porter with her own money purchased 120 acres at the southwest end of the lake and built a second, greatly expanded, version of the first cabin in Geneva. The home took two years to build, and Mrs. Porter bought a cottage across the lake where she spent the summers supervising the construction of the house and starting work on the needed tree surgery and on her wildflower preserve. She also spent the winter of 1912–13 as a boarder in a neighboring farm home.[32]

The second Limberlost cabin at Rome City contained some twenty rooms, including, most importantly, a professional darkroom. It was located on a fourteen-acre plot of dense woodland bordering the lake. Mrs. Porter expanded her holding until she eventually owned 150 acres with two miles of shoreline. This acreage she named "Wildflower Woods." At Wildflower Woods she continued her prolific writing, completing three novels, one nature book, a children's book, and innumerable magazine articles.

But by 1916 the same ravages which had destroyed the Limberlost in Adams County were to threaten the new Limberlost around Wildflower Woods in Noble County. Drainage ditches were planned and were actually cut, lowering the levels of the natural lakes so abundant in the region. Fortunately, Sylvan Lake was a man-made lake and was little affected by the drainage project. Its immediate area and particularly the swampy portion of her holdings were safe from destruction. And so it was that when her efforts to oppose the drainage project failed, she began her frantic struggle to move to the protection of her own land for its preservation all the native flora she possibly could. She had selected her site with the thought in mind that it represented the best of swamp and forest and lakeland. She had planned from the start to concentrate in one area the widely scattered flowers, shrubs, and trees which in nature are not so concentrated, and she had worked consistently but not hurriedly toward this goal. But now, destruction was imminent, and she worked frantically:

I had known that I must hurry, that I must gather all the beautiful things I could that lay in the way of clearing and draining on the individual land of each farmer who wanted to increase his tillable area, but I had not thought that anyone would seriously contemplate so devastating such a fair heritage from God as to run a great ditch through my working territory that would dry up each spring and brook of running water, that would dry up most of the wells, and lower the surface of the lakes from seven to, in some instances, nine and ten feet, depending on the contour of the land.

When I found that such a scheme had definitely gone through, that plans were being made that only the most stringent and immediate work could save Noble County, I was horrified. Drying up the springs, drying up the streams, and lowering the lake meant to exterminate that growth by running water, meant to kill the great trees that had flourished since the beginning of time around the borders of the lakes, meant to kill the vines and shrubs and bushes, the ferns and the iris and the water hyacinths, the arrowhead lilies and the rosemary and the orchids, and it meant, too, that men were madly and recklessly doing an insane thing without really understanding what they were doing.[33]

How well she fought can be seen by the visitor to Wildflower Woods. More than half a century after her death, many of the plants she brought in have established themselves and are found in a greater profusion than in almost any other section of the state.

As the work of Gene Stratton Porter became known and her reading public became aware of the conservancy project at Wildflower Woods, people began to send her plant materials from all over the world. With her mother's fine sense for plant propagation and with her own knowledge of habitats of plants, she attempted to establish these foreigners in the climate of

Indiana. With some she succeeded; with some she failed. But the urgency to preserve native species was uppermost in her mind and compelled her activity. "Life became one round of fight. Fight from morning until night. Fight for the war, fight for the conservation of physical and spiritual comfort and of hunt, seek, and search to rescue every one of these delicate little blossoms possible before destruction overtook them."[34]

It was Gene Stratton Porter's task to record the passing of the swamp, not to engage in a futile struggle to save it. For the swamp furnished the materials to instill in people an appreciation of fine woods to be used in their homes. The two homes in Indiana which Mrs. Porter constructed for herself even today reflect the love for fine woods and their durability as a source of lasting pleasure. But this was daring in itself in that the period was one of painted plaster and wallpaper. Mrs. Porter was a level-headed realist who knew that civilization must be served; the preservation of all nature in its pristine state would leave no room for the growth and development of the nation. It is, of course, lamentable that the principles of conservation—the harvesting rather than the destruction—which could have preserved, at least in part, this region were not employed.

It is interesting to note that the direct idea of conservation does appear in the earliest magazine articles, in the California novels, and in certain essays, and one might speculate as to what position she might have taken in future novels were it not for her untimely death in 1924.

VII *War and California*

In 1917–18, Gene Stratton Porter endured World War I at the Cabin at Rome City. She seems to have been little affected by the conflict. Of course, she suffered the privation and the heartaches of the war, but she wrote little for or about it, as one might have expected from the pen of the foremost woman writer of the time. In fact, no magazine articles have come to light which were published during the war years. A letter of the time mentions that she was requested by an Indianapolis paper to write an article telling how women could earn money in their homes to buy Liberty Bonds.[35] Perhaps she did other newspaper writing in support of the war effort.

The war does not feature to any extent in the novels with the exception of *The Keeper of the Bees,* which has for its hero a wounded veteran. The war is over when the novel begins, and it is only the protagonist's effort to recover from it that makes the book in any sense a war novel.

In 1919 Gene Stratton Porter made her first trip to California. Again the reasons are not clear or are twofold. "I loved this location [Indiana] and should have remained there to live and die *had not the question of help become utterly impossible in the country.*" But a few sentences later she says, "The war was a horrible thing, and I ended by breaking down with the flu with no nurse and a doctor forty miles away. In desperation I fled to California."[36] But be it from ill health or from the lack of household help, Gene Stratton Porter did go to California and did establish her permanent home there. At first, it was winters in California and summers in Indiana, but by 1923 the determination to make California her year-round home had become fixed. She purchased land on Catalina Island and in the Los Angeles suburb of Bel Air and started the construction of a summer home and "workshop" on the island and a winter, or permanent, home on her "baby mountain" overlooking the city and the ocean. The island house was completed and occupied for one season; the mainland home was not yet finished at her death. That popular writing in the first quarter of the twentieth century was not only popular but profitable can be established by the fact that each of these homes cost in the neighborhood of a half million dollars.

On the evening of December 6, 1924, the Lincoln limousine in which Gene Stratton Porter was being driven to visit her brother Jerome Stratton was struck by a trolley car. She was fatally injured and died without regaining consciousness. She was interred in a mausoleum in Hollywood Memorial Cemetery.

The few years spent in California wrought a great change in the life-style of Gene Stratton Porter. No longer isolated, she became gregarious and much interested in the people as well as the scene of her new land. She became social. For the first time in her life she was in close proximity with people of wealth, culture, and talent, and of artistic appreciation. Her position as the country's foremost woman author (plus her riches) won her ready acceptance in the social circles of Los Angeles. Because of her active involvement in the production of films (she had formed her own company) she moved freely through the motion picture colony. And she became civic minded to the extent that she was active in the women's clubs which were becoming quite powerful throughout the country; she was often a speaker at their larger conventions, and she attempted to enlist their aid in her cause of the moment—her fight for decency in the movies.[37]

As full and as rewarding as her life in California had become, Mrs. Porter never lost her deep and abiding interest in nature, and the Pacific landscape was as varied as the Indiana scene had been limited. But Porter set out to know and to conquer it and to report it for her readers. Only two of her books, *Her Father's Daughter* and *The Keeper of the Bees*, have California settings, but in each of them the new background is drawn in equally fine detail, as was the Limberlost. The fact that her last novel, *The Magic Garden*, is not set in California seems only proof that it had its conception if not its inception long before the move to California.

After the arrival in California, there is little mention of field work and no reference to the photographing of birds. Perhaps Porter was too busily engaged in her new social life and too occupied with her building projects to find the time for her favorite pursuits. Perhaps the study of California birds was postponed until the new life settled into place. At any rate Gene Stratton Porter seems to have been more interested in the prolific plant life around her than in the birds. Had she lived, there might have come studies as minute and as detailed as those of the Limberlost days.

But she did not live: Death intervened.

CHAPTER 2

The Careers That Grew
Out of a Life

I Novelist and Naturalist

GENE Stratton Porter never considered herself a novelist.
She maintained that her books were all nature studies
"sugar-coated with fiction" so that they would appeal to the
great reading public. But such is not quite the case. Since a novel
is only a fictional prose narrative of considerable length, the
books are novels. And while nature does play a large part in all
but one of them, it is the story that carries them along. And
nature is not the story. One possible exception is her first book,
The Song of the Cardinal, in which a pair of red birds—cardinal
grosbeaks—are the protagonists, and nature *is* the story. But
Porter considered this among her nature books, not among the
novels. She thought of *Freckles* as her first novel.[1]

An extremely accurate and detailed natural history furnishes
the setting in which the plots of the stories unfold. Perhaps any
enduring fame due Gene Stratton Porter as a novelist must rest
on these descriptions of a scene pretty much vanished from
American life, but it is the story itself—superimposed on this
background—which carries the reader along through the pages
of such depictions. There are educationally sound, well-reasoned
and well-researched affirmations of nature in the context of her
stories. But often there was no need for research; she *knew* the
nature of which she wrote. One reviewer recognized this quality
and reported that "when dealing with the glories of the swamp
flora or the mysteries of bird-music, the author shows
undiminished power in that better direction."[2]

Porter was achievement oriented; her books were designed on
the basis of providing sheer entertainment for her readers and as

a vehicle for sales on the open market. While nature was predominant in all the books, Porter realized that it was entertainment which would make the books sell and disseminate her nature lore to the widest possible audience. By some standards of criticism there was indeed a poverty of literary value, but the books made a genuine appeal to many who might otherwise be non-readers. These were the readers of light, romantic fiction; these were—in large part—the readers of the women's magazines.

One of the qualities which made Gene Stratton Porter so immensely popular with the readers of her day was the ease with which they could associate themselves with her characters. For the most part, the problems encountered were everyday problems—disappointments, tensions, dissatisfactions, even pleasures—requiring only the same constant adjustment necessary for everday living. And the solution to these problems often required only hard work and ennobling contacts with nature.[3] Porter's characters achieve economic success perhaps in response to the biblical injunction, "Seek ye first the kingdom of God and His righteousness and all these other things shall be added unto you."

Much of Porter's appeal is the appeal of the Great American Dream as exemplified in rags-to-riches stories of the Horatio Alger type in which success, distinction, honor, and wealth are the rewards of persistent ambition and hard work. A century has passed since Alger's books were written, but American optimism as portrayed in the mass media—especially in women's magazines and daytime television soap operas—remains undiminished.

II Themes

The novels of Gene Stratton Porter as complete units are all predictable variations of the same pattern—the overcoming of obstacles through goodness and determination.[4] Almost all the major plots play upon this motif, and it is present to a greater or lesser degree in the subplots as well. It is seen most clearly in *Freckles*, in *A Girl of the Limberlost*, in *Michael O'Halloran*, and in *The White Flag*. Its operation is less obvious in *The Harvester*, *Laddie*, and *At the Foot of the Rainbow*.

Several themes derive from this primary pattern. Perhaps the overriding motivation of all Porter novels can be stated in terms of the struggle of a man and a woman for happiness. It is hard to find one of the books in which this theme is not evident either in plot or subplot. It is, of course, the main story line in *Freckles*, in *A Girl of the Limberlost*, and in *The Harvester*. It becomes minor only in *Michael O'Halloran* with the subplots of the Minturns and the Hardings and is somewhat overshadowed by the strong attraction between the two male characters of *At the Foot of the Rainbow*. Kate Bates in *A Daughter of the Land* seems to be working out her destiny alone, or in spite of the interference of men, but in the final pages of the book the real hero emerges.

An offshoot of the above theme is what might be termed the woman-as-prize theme. This aspect is clearly presented in *Freckles*, where the Swamp Angel epitomizes all that is desirable for the hero if only he were by birth and by wealth worthy of winning such a reward. The theme is doubly established in *A Girl of the Limberlost*, both in the main plot and in a subplot. Elnora Comstock and Edith Carr are presented as prizeworthy, and conflict develops between plot and subplot at the point where Philip Ammon must decide which prize is more desirable.[5]

A third variation on the main theme is that of certain triumph-over-adversity or the premise that happiness grows out of adversity. The prime illustration is again Elnora Comstock who achieves her final happiness as a result of overcoming one difficulty after another. Elnora differs from Mahala Spellman in *The White Flag* in that Elnora's is a series of small triumphs while Mahala suffers defeat after defeat until the culminating victory. Mickey O'Halloran, of course, triumphs time and time again, and the theme is worked well into the ground of many of the other novels.

There are other themes of less importance but still essential and reoccurring in the novels of Gene Stratton Porter. It must be noted, however, that these others are all subsidiary to the main pattern of the overcoming of obstacles through goodness and determination. In fact, the subsidiary theme may generate or may *be* the obstacle to be overcome.

One such theme is the clouded past, quite frequently the obscured birthright. This theme is predominant in *Freckles*, in *The Harvester*, and in *Laddie*. Freckles cannot achieve happiness because of his orphan state and his total ignorance of his parentage. Rather melodramatically, Porter puts it that he must know or die. He knows and does not die. He is of noble birth and quite worthy of the Angel. A slightly different use is made of the obscured past in *The Harvester*. Having rescued Ruth from an environment of deepest destitution and privation, David Langston cannot rest until he finds her very affluent grandparents and proves to himself that, if Ruth ever comes to love him, it will certainly not be from need. He quite nearly loses, but, true to a Porter novel, everything comes out right in the end. The operation of the birthright theme has a still different application in *Laddie*. The Stantons know perfectly well who they are, but their claim to an English title is not known to the Pryors. While it would, perhaps, be of no consequence to the Princess, it is of utmost consequence to her father and eases the path to the happy marriage ending the book.

The clouded past also touches *A Girl of the Limberlost* and *The Keeper of the Bees*, but not quite to the same extent that it does the previously mentioned novels. Elnora Comstock is disturbed by the lack of knowledge of her dead father, but revelation is finally made to her, and even more importantly to her mother. Kate Comstock's reaction to the knowledge that her husband had been unfaithful to her and she unjust to her daughter borders on the sensational, but it makes good reading and aids in the resolution of the main conflict. In *The Keeper of the Bees* the clouded past centers around the mystery of the Storm Girl and the mixed-up identities that follow. Here it is only ignorance on the part of Jamie MacFarlane—a lack of knowledge—which when finally resolved leads to the happy ending of the book.

Another obstacle that Gene Stratton Porter puts into many of her novels is the mortal illness (and recovery) of a principal character. The mortal illness figures in *Freckles, The Harvester, A Girl of the Limberlost*, and *The White Flag* and to a lesser extent in other novels. Once more, Freckles is the most prominent victim. He is badly crushed by a falling tree in a valiant and successful effort to save the Angel, and the struggle for his life fills many pages. The same lengthy involvement is true of Ruth in *The Harvester* and of Philip Ammon in *A Girl of the Limberlost*. Another aspect almost worthy of being called a theme in itself is the lack of a will to live. Freckles does not want to live without the knowledge that he is worthy of the Angel; Ruth lacks the will to live without being sure of the resolution of the conflict between her love and her duty. Philip is devoid of the desire for life if he has lost Elnora. There is a slight difference in *The White Flag* in that Mahala rather than lacking the will to live is so oppressed by life that her battle against typhoid seems helpless. At least twice, the mortal illness *is* mortal. The only resolution of the triangle of *At the Foot of the Rainbow* is possible through the death of Jimmy Malone. And in *The Keeper of the Bees,* Jamie's supposed wife dies in childbirth. There are other death scenes, of course, especially in *The White Flag* and in *A Daughter of the Land,* where Porter seems able to resolve her plots only by killing off threatening characters, but they do not quite fit the mortal illness theme.

It is interesting to note at this point that Gene Stratton Porter utilized the actual death of her oldest sister, Katherine Marshall, which she described in a letter to another sister, Ada Wilson,[6] almost word for word in *The Keeper of the Bees.*[7] This sweetly sentimental account is in keeping with the telling of the burial of the two mothers in *The Harvester.*[8]

Another favorite theme of Gene Stratton Porter's is the dream or vision come to life. This theme is the prime motivation for *The Harvester.* David sees the vision of the Dream Girl so clearly that he builds a house for her and sets about finding her, never doubting for a moment the reality of his dream. Elnora sees her dead father in a dream; he is playing a violin, and the same violin and music become a part of her life. This dream is also responsible for Kate Comstock's coming to her senses through the discovery of her husband's infidelity. There is a curious half-dream, half-reality appearance of the Storm Girl in *The Keeper of the Bees.*

Perhaps more of a technique than a real theme is the employment of coincidence or happenstance in many of the novels. The prime example is that of the O'Mores in *Freckles,* who just happen to be in America searching for clues to the lost heir after eighteen years. There is the almost parallel instance of the grandparents' finding of Ruth after almost the same interval of time in *The Harvester.*

Another important use of coincidence occurs in *The Keeper of the Bees.* Jamie MacFarlane just happens to pass the Beekeeper's house at the exact moment of his being stricken, just happens to be free of all ties so that he can take the Beekeeper's place, and just happens to fit right into the life-style of the Beekeeper and into the affection of the Little Scout. The most marring use of coincidence occurs in *The White Flag,* where an impossible situation has evolved. Jason and Mahala discover their real love, but Jason has married Ellen, who bore him the son which should have been Mahala's. Ellen is conveniently struck by lightning, and Mahala and Jason get each other and the baby.

Running through the novels with a frequency almost sufficient to make it thematic is the notion of the unfortunate marriage. It is in *Freckles, The Harvester, A Girl of the Limberlost, The White Flag,* and above all in *A Daughter of the Land.* In the first three books, the unfortunate marriage has taken place before the story opens and is responsible for the difficulty encountered by the offspring of these marriages. In *Freckles* and in *The Harvester* this motif is coupled with the notion of lost parents and obscured identity. Mickey and Peaches of *Michael O'Halloran* probably fit into both categories. In *The Keeper of the Bees* and in *A Girl of the Limberlost,* the idea is handled differently. The lack of marriage and the subsequent "marriage" results in the birth of Jamie MacFarlane, Junior, and in the death of the mother. It would be hard to call the marriage of Kate Comstock anything but unfortunate, yet without it there would have been no Elnora and no story. But perhaps the most unfortunate marriage of all was that of Mary Malone in *At the Foot of the Rainbow.* Here is a loveless marriage founded on trickery and keeping two rightful lovers apart. It is a Miles Standish–John Alden sort of thing with a reverse twist; Jimmy Malone did speak for himself and lied about Mary's response. With the moral code of Gene Stratton Porter's time, which was of course that of her readers, the only resolution of the predicament is for Jimmy to die. Kate Bates's marriage to George Holt in *A Daughter of the Land* was unfortunate in the extreme, but she went into it with her eyes wide open and deserves little sympathy for the outcome.

The life that gave rise to a career was the life of a home builder and home maker, and these occupations figure with almost thematic regularity in the novels. Gene Stratton Porter built three homes and was engaged in the building of a fourth at the time of her death. There is much building, rebuilding, decorating, and redecorating in the novels. Outstanding, of course, is the building of the house in *The Harvester.* With her usual inclination to draw from her own life, the Harvester's house is her own home in Geneva. It is not all there, but the parts that are described are faithful. But the setting for the house and for

the story is not Geneva, but Rome City! Perhaps the intent to
remove to Sylvan Lake was in Porter's mind long before the
recorded materialization. Frank N. Wallace, who was Porter's
tree surgeon and who became her chief assistant in the
establishment of Wildflower Woods, and who married her
secretary, Lorene Miller, places her intention as being formed as
early as 1909 rather than 1913. *The Harvester* was published in
1911.[9]

Other home-making passages occur throughout the books.
Kate Comstock refurbishes her cabin and rents and redecorates
a house. Mary Malone completely redoes her home after Jimmy
Malone's death. The Hardings in *Michael O'Halloran* build a new
home out of the old with particular attention to the kitchen,
which is an almost exact duplicate of Mrs. Porter's own kitchen in
Rome City. Linda Strong makes over a part of the house she
shares with her sister. But in all these cases, Gene Stratton Porter
is writing actual descriptions of her own homes—in Indiana or
California—and putting her ideas of construction and decoration
into the minds of her characters. In *The Magic Garden* the
rebuilding of the Forrester's cottage is of a different stamp; it
seems as if Porter relied solely on her imagination rather than
her experience in her refurbishing of this dwelling, and her
attempt at opulence lacks the convincingness of her descriptions
of simpler dwellings. She wrote best what she knew best.

House building—in addition to Linda Strong's efforts—plays a
large part in *Her Father's Daughter*. Marian Thorne is trying to
make her way in the world as an architect, and she designs a
"perfect home" for an architectural competition. The plans are
purloined, the thief wins the contest, and an interesting subplot
develops. But for present purposes, once again the plans and the
setting are those of the home Porter was dreaming over and
planning to construct for herself once she secured her "baby
mountain" in the Los Angeles suburb of Bel Air.

In a magazine article written for *Country Life in America* as
part of a series, "My Ideal Home," Gene Stratton Porter
described her own ideal home. The descriptions of the interiors
are simply those of the two Indiana cabins she built—expanded
and refined as if there were no limitations of space or money.
The Indiana homes, maintained by the state as memorials to the
author, are unfortunately (especially the one in Geneva) late
bastard Victorian in style. The color drawing made in 1921 by

architectural artist Francis Keally from Porter's description is
thoroughly modern even by late-twentieth-century standards.[10]

It is impossible to separate the naturalist from the novelist in
the writing of Gene Stratton Porter. This does not mean that a
classification of the works into novels and nature books has not or
cannot be done. This book does it, her publishers did it, and
Porter herself did it. But the naturalist writes through the fiction
of the novels, and the novelist writes narratives into the nature
books. Fascinating stories are to be found in *Tales You Won't
Believe* and in *Homing with the Birds* in particular. The story of
the search for rare orchids blends narrative, description, and
pathos into its makeup.[11] Sometimes the naturalist merely muses
or reports—especially if her intent borders on the scientific—but
more often the method is anecdotal, simple storytelling.

The books of the naturalist are narrowly outnumbered by
those of the storyteller—there are twelve novels as opposed to
eight nature titles. But three of these are reissues or new editions
of earlier publication. However, nature was the preeminent
interest of Gene Stratton Porter, and nature permeates all of the
novels with the possible exception of *The White Flag*. It is used as
background, as motivation for action, and for the shaping of
character. The nature books also provided the outlet for that
other, and perhaps chief talent Porter possessed, the discerning
eye which made her photographs and illustrations outstanding.
The novels did not lend themselves to photographic illustration;
only *The Song of the Cardinal* is replete with illustrations from
the author's own camera. But the nature books are chock full of
pictures of subjects who responded to Mrs. Porter's painstakingly
patient approach to the photographing of nature. As one
reviewer wrote, "Her work . . . is worthy of high praise for the
excellence of many of her photographic studies; only a field
student who is adept with the camera can appreciate how fine
some of these pictures really are."[12]

However, it is hard to deny that Porter's career as a novelist is
the most important one engendered by her life, for it supported
all the others. The novels paid the way for the less popular
books, which were Porter's favorites and which carried her
message of nature.[13] She was wily enough to insert her doctrine
into the novels and thus assure its widest possible reception.
Through her wide and loyal readership she spread the gospel of

nature to millions who would never read the great naturalists or who would find them dull.

III   *Magazine Contributor*

Gene Stratton Porter is usually, and rightly so, thought of as a novelist, for it was the novels that sold in the millions. But she was much more diverse as has been noted. It was her intention that for each novel she wrote she would also produce a book of what she called "natural history." That this plan did not quite come about was due to her branching out into other nonprofitable fields, into poetry and children's books. In addition to being a busy novelist, she was a prolific magazine writer, an illustrator of her own books, and in later years a producer of motion pictures.

One hundred seventy-one separate magazine publications by Gene Stratton Porter have been discovered. Of these, forty-nine are serializations of novels or nature writing which later achieved book status. Eight are poems, including the long serialized *Euphorbia.* There are six short stories, four of which are chapters from novels. The remainder is divided among six camera department notes, seventy-two editorials or editorial narratives, ten general articles, and twenty nature articles not reprinted. Only sixty-five of the entire 171 articles did not see subsequent publication in one or more of her books, and many of these sixty-five appear in part in later work. Gene Stratton Porter was one inclined to use and reuse the materials she gathered.

Because of its impermanence, the magazine writing of a popular author would ordinarily have no place in a volume of this sort. But it is impossible to dismiss the writing that Gene Stratton Porter did for periodicals. There are several reasons for this judgment. First, the magazine articles, especially the early ones, contain some of the finest nature writing that Porter did. Second, the articles reveal a great deal about the life of the author—material which is not found in other sources. Third, the articles are more conservation oriented than are the novels or the nature books themselves. Finally, in the magazine articles are to be found the roots of much of the material which appears in the books.

The early magazine articles that Gene Stratton Porter wrote,

especially those for *Outing,* contain some of the best nature
writing that she did. This claim is valid because these articles are
presented straightforwardly without any sentimentality or
attempts to humanize the birds. They contain accurate descriptions of bird life presented interestingly and with highly original
and scrupulously correct photographs of birds and bird families.
For the most part the early articles were reportorial. "Bird
Architecture," the first *Outing* article in July 1901, is straightforward expository writing, dealing with birds' nests and especially
with the materials birds use and the ways they employ them. The
presentation is clear and only occasionally anecdotal, as it is
when she tells of the robin's nest at Limberlost Cabin in Geneva
and of the bell-bird's nest constructed of roots instead of the
usual twigs and fibers.[14]

In the articles published in both *Recreation* and *Outing,* the
pattern is simply one of relating experiences with birds and
illustrating with photographs of particular charm and excellence.
In the camera department she conducted for *Recreation,* she
told others how to make good pictures, basing her advice on her
own experiences.

These early articles are almost entirely devoid of sentimentality and the anthropomorphism which marks much of the later
nature work. One exception is found in "The Birds' Kindergarten" of April 1902. In this article she does humanize in
that she likens the education of nestlings to the early education
of children and attributes human characteristics to the bird
mother. She takes issue with naturalists and ornithologists who
attribute everything to instinct and makes a great point of the
importance of training in the raising of the young. The rest of the
Outing articles follow the pattern of the first one mentioned;
they are exact and detailed accounts of the life habits—
particularly the nesting and brooding habits—of birds or of the
adventures and difficulties confronting the author in her
attempts to secure her photographs.

Most of these early writings occur in whole or in part in the
nature work or in the novels of Gene Stratton Porter. The story
of the Black Vulture is perhaps the most recurring of all. It
appears in *What I Have Done with Birds,* in *Friends in Feathers,*
and in *Homing with the Birds;* and it is a large part of the novel
Freckles. In fact the working title for *Freckles* was *The Falling*

Feather and refers to the incident of a vulture's feather drifting down the sky, thus leading to the discovery of the nest.[15]

Porter based all of her nature writing on her actual experience in the field. Endowed with unlimited determination and patience, she achieved remarkable success. These stories of her encounters with nature, coupled with the excellent photography accompanying them, did much to establish Gene Stratton Porter with a wide circle of readers, so that she was not an unknown when her books began to appear. She advocated that her readers do as she had done; if the camera was not their medium, they could at least go out into the fields and woods and see and observe as had she. In an interview she told how it could be done: "The only way to love nature is to live close to it until you have learned its pathless travel, growth, and inhabitants. As you know the fields, you must begin at the gate and find your way slowly, else you will not hear the great secret and see the compelling vision. How many people know anything about moths? There are trees you never before have seen, flowers and vines the botanists fail to mention, and such music as your ears cannot hear elsewhere."[16]

The articles which appeared in magazines before the publication of her first book are first-person accounts of her affair with nature. The reader glimpses the writer, sees her at work, and becomes acquainted with her habits and characteristics. The Bird Woman who appears as a character in *Freckles, A Girl of the Limberlost,* and *The Harvester,* and who is obviously Gene Stratton Porter herself, is first introduced in "The Real Babes in the Woods" in *Metropolitan Magazine* for August 1902. This story has the Bird Woman comforting a boy who objects to the death of the children in the fairy tale by telling him of the real babes in the woods—the nestlings—and of the excellent care given them by their mothers. In all her appearances in the books, the Bird Woman appears to be single—at least there is never any mention of husband or family. Meehan makes it plain that her father was indefatigable in his efforts to help Gene Stratton Porter in her ventures into the swamp.[17] The situation is further complicated by "The Real Babes in the Woods," which states that the frightened boy should have been the Bird Woman's son, but that she had renounced his father in order to continue her work. No one denies the right of the fiction writer to indulge in fantasy, but when the writer is depicting an autobiographical character, one wonders at least about the psychological implications.

The first short stories that Gene Stratton Porter wrote and sold to *Metropolitan Magazine* were "Laddie, the Princess, and the Pie" in September 1901, followed closely by "How Laddie and the Princess Spelled Down at the Christmas Bee" as the lead story in the Christmas issue of the same year. From the titles it is apparent that these stories are of the same autobiographical stamp as *Laddie*, the novel. As a matter of fact, each appears intact in the novel, leading to conjecture as to whether or not Porter had written *Laddie* in its entirety before these publications or whether the novel grew out of these short stories. The second "Laddie" story almost *had* to be written before Mrs. Porter accepted the commission for it. She was not aware of the publication of the first story before the September issue of *Metropolitan* came out. She wrote the editor and received a reply—at least a week would have elapsed, considering the mail service of the early 1900s. She tells that she had just a day and a half to complete her manuscript, including photographs.[18] But these *Metropolitan* stories, along with the *Recreation* and *Outing* series and with many more which were to come later, do reveal a great deal about the author. These references and allusions permit the reader to fill in many gaps which Meehan and other writers leave unstopped in the biography of Gene Stratton Porter.

Much that is known of the life of Gene Stratton Porter comes from the autobiographical material she prepared for *Chambers Journal* (London) in 1914 and for the London *Bookman* in 1916, and which was issued in part in the *Ladies' Home Journal* also in 1916. But there are other articles which give glimpses of the author's life. "What My Father Meant to Me," from the *American Magazine* is particularly revealing of the closeness between father and daughter and of the sacrifices he made for her.[19] "Why I Always Wear My Rose Colored Glasses," also from the *American*, justifies Porter's confirmed optimism with incidents from her life.[20] She tells of the vicissitudes as well as the joys of childhood and how always looking on the best side of things helped overcome sorrow and pain. She makes the inaccurate statement that "he [Leander], my mother and my sister were all laid to rest during the same year."[21] Actually,

Leander died in 1872, Mary Stratton in 1875, and Anastasia Stratton Taylor in 1882. Again, the writer has license, but the reader must beware of accepting too readily autobiography which is not plainly labeled autobiography.

By 1905 the magazine articles and her first book, *The Song of the Cardinal,* had established Gene Stratton Porter as one of the leading nature writers of the country. The energetic and aspiring Edward W. Bok, editor of the *Ladies' Home Journal,* eager to secure this new talent for his magazine, arranged to meet with her in Chicago to persuade her to do a series of bird articles for him. This was an opportunity for Porter to tap the large audience represented by the *Journal's* circulation. Perhaps Bok had been influenced by the success of "Freckles' Chickens," a chapter from the novel which had appeared in the *Journal* in the November 1904 issue shortly after the book was published. At any rate, the arrangement seemed mutually advantageous, and the first installment of *What I Have Done with Birds* appeared in April of 1906; the series was concluded in the August issue of the same year. With such a propitious beginning, it is hard to understand why there were no more articles written for the *Ladies' Home Journal* with the exception of the sketch of her life previously mentioned.

Porter had twenty-eight appearances in *Good Housekeeping.* The first two were short poems appearing in January and May of 1921, and the last was an article on poetry in April of 1925. The other publications are accounted for by three serializations—of *Euphorbia, The White Flag,* and *Tales You Won't Believe.* It is interesting to note that in February of 1925 Gene Stratton Porter was being serialized simultaneously in *Good Housekeeping* and in *McCall's.*

Perhaps the magazine articles which give the most insight into the life and character of Gene Stratton Porter are the long series of editorials she wrote for *McCall's Magazine.* Meehan relates how her mother was approached for a series of editorials by Harry B. Burton, the new editor of *McCall's,* how Mrs. Porter was attracted to him, and how she hoped to help him make *McCall's* a top-ranking woman's magazine. She wrote of this hope in a letter to Mr. Nelson Doubleday:

There is something about Burton of *McCall's,* possibly that thing called "personality" that makes a deep appeal to me. He is a brilliant chap, clean as a ribbon, and if he is not a live wire, I do not know that article when I see it. And he is going straight ahead. His last issue of McCall's was fine. You could scarcely beat his list of authors, and he holds them to absolutely clean, sane stuff, not oversexed, and not tainted with the spirit of jazz and exaggeration which rules so much of the material that is being put out today. I take extreme pride in the way that magazine has grown during the past three years, and I hope that we shall be able to go until we put *McCall's* at the top of American publications, just for the sake of having the fun of putting over something worth while. It is clean as a whistle, full of vivid, interesting things, and it belongs to the people who are living as you and I live.[22]

It is evident that Mrs. Porter took an active and personal interest in the writing that she did for Harry Burton and for *McCall's*.

Not wanting to interrupt her larger writing by stopping to do each editorial page shortly before it was due, Gene Stratton Porter formed the habit of writing at least a year's supply in advance. At the time of her death in December 1924, *McCall's* announced (in its issue of January 1925) that Mrs. Porter had sent them enough material for "Gene Stratton-Porter's Page" to last through 1926. But there were more, and the final appearance of this feature was not until the issue of December 1927, and a selection from these pages makes up the content of the posthumous volume of essays, *Let Us Highly Resolve*.

The third aspect of the magazine writing of Gene Stratton Porter worthy of consideration is conservation. In everything that she wrote concerning nature and the outdoors, the idea of conservation is either explicit or implicit. As has been noted, her very first work to be published in *Recreation* was a tirade against the destruction of birds for their plumage. And the notion continues throughout her work even until the final essay, "Shall We Save Our Natural Beauty?" in the posthumous *Let Us Highly Resolve*.

Conservation early became an interest and an aim in the life of Gene Stratton Porter. Her childhood on Hopewell Farm had firmly fixed the love of nature—of both plants and animals—as a guiding force in her life. While the magazine articles not reprinted in books are infrequently devoted to conservation per se, the abiding love of nature they preach includes the idea of preservation along with appreciation. Even the depiction of her ideal home in *Country Life* presents the notion of conservation in that for her a home depends as much on its natural setting as it does on its architecture and decoration. She is quite modern in her suggestion that a home should be expanded into the outdoors surrounding it.[23] The same notion persists in her factual account of the Nebraska ranch she visited and reported on for *Country Life.* There must be maintained a reciprocal and working balance between agriculture and nature.[24]

The magazine writing of Gene Stratton Porter was, therefore, an important part of the career that grew out of the life. Much of the writing that saw subsequent publication between the covers of books—including parts of the novels themselves—first appeared in the periodicals of the day. The materials not recurring in book form, especially the occasional pieces written for *McCall's,* reveal a great deal about the life, the habits, and the opinions of the author. These pieces show her to be sagacious, kindly, and well fitted to be the spokeswoman for the vast audience of middle-class Americans she represented. Perhaps she did not mold public opinion, but she reflected the moral viewpoint and social standards of a large following, less vocal and ill-equipped to express itself. She became, as William Lyon Phelps put it "a public institution, like Yellowstone Park."[25]

IV Poet

Gene Stratton Porter was not a great poet and yet she attempted to be and considered herself to be one. As she grew older, she began to covet a place of greatness for her writing and especially for her poetry. She wrote that she was willing for time to be the ultimate judge of her work and that she was sure time would vindicate her own belief in her greatness. Resenting the adverse criticism of her novels of which she said, "I am desperately tired. . .of having the high grade literary critics of the country give a second- and at times a third-class rating to my literary work because I would not write of complexes and rank materialism, which is another name for adultery," she saw no obstacle to her becoming a top-ranking poet. She continued, "However, there is no reason why I should not make a first-grade literary reputation with poetry, which has been an obsession with me from childhood and which I have studied all my life in an effort to fit myself for such work.[26]

The major poetic works of Gene Stratton Porter are four: *The*

Fire Bird, Euphorbia, Jesus of the Emerald, and *Whitmore's Bull.*
The minor works consist of short poems, some published in
periodicals and some scattered through her books. *Morning
Face,* the book she wrote for her granddaughter, contains much
of the verse she wrote for children. These minor poems need not
detain the reader. They are light, and for the most part pleasing
verse, but they take their place with thousands of other light and
pleasing verses and have no claim either to poetry or to
permanence. The following is a fair example:

Blue Eyed Mary

When winter's chill has scarce left earth
    And April winds blow "Hey down derry!"
Comes gaily dancing down my hill
    Sweet, laughing, blue-eyed Mary.

She wears a dress of bronzy green
    Draped round her light and airy
She lifts the loveliest face I've seen
    Brave, tender, blue-eyed Mary.

Her eyes shine like the azure sky,
    Her step light as a fairy;
Her face, no crystal drift so white
    Dear, steadfast, blue-eyed Mary.

My hat is off to Bouncing Bet
    Gill-over-the-ground runs quite contrary
Black-eyed Susan is my pet,
    But I'm in love with blue-eyed Mary.[27]

The attempt, as in the final stanza, to insert too much nature into
her lyric mars the result.

The major poetic works are worthy of some consideration.
While they do not succeed as poetry, they invariably succeed as
story, and as story they are among the best work Porter did. The
restrictions of poetry—although never mastered—forced the
author to compress and discipline her narratives. Their relative
shortness, as compared with the wordiness of the novels,
demanded a severe pruning of extraneous materials.

The Firebird was the first of Porter's books of poetry, discounting, of course, the verse which had appeared in *Morning Face*. *The Firebird* tells the story of an Indian princess, Yiada, who by her wiles has led her rival, Coüy-Oüy, to her death. She made three attempts—one by leading her into the path of a venomous snake, one by drawing her dangerously close to the den of a female bear, and one by luring her into a treacherous quicksand in search of water lilies. This last subterfuge is successful. Yiada is forced to flee her tribe and finds refuge and a husband among her mother's people, the Mandanas. She bears three children, only to have each of them die by one of the same means she had attempted against the life of Coüy-Oüy. The whole poem is concerned with Yiada's plea to the Medicine Man to make her a strong medicine that will ease her guilty conscience.

The Firebird has an almost perfect balance and antithesis; its plan is worthy of a masterful poem. It is in the lines themselves that the poetry fails. Gene Stratton Porter claimed that it was not poetry in the ordinary sense but free verse. "For the great part the text is written in the rhythm of the deep forest, but there are times when the wash of the sea and the winds of the canyons predominate."[28] If this were only true, perhaps *The Firebird* might have become the great Indian epic she hoped and claimed it would be. But Porter was not the master of these rhythms. She had not the genius of a John Gould Fletcher, who could build a whole series of poems on varied and subtle rhythms such as she imagined she was using.

Porter appeared not to know that free verse is not verse that takes any desired liberties with established poetic forms. Her models were usually very simple lyric patterns, but she seemed to lack an inborn sense of meter, syllable, and accent. Take for example the eight-line poem with which Jeannette Meehan chose to end her book about her mother:

> Come with me, and you shall know
> The Garden where God's flowers grow.
> Come with me, and you shall hear
> His waters whisper songs of cheer.
>
> And if you lift your eyes on high

> To see the larks fly in the sky,
> Let them rove on to the Heavens above
> And meet the miracle of God's love.

Gene Stratton Porter had the inspiration but not the ear or the craftsman's patience for poetry.

A short passage from *The Firebird* will illustrate both the genius and the shortcomings of the work. The Firebird of the title is, of course, Gene Stratton Porter's beloved cardinal, and she recounts the Indian legend of how he got his red coat. After the flood, there remained on earth only the Great Sachem, his wife, and one pair of every bird and beast. But there was no fire. The Sachem sent a beaver to the underworld to get a coal from the campfires of the dark spirits, but the beaver burned his mouth and dropped it. A mountain lion searched the earth, but there was no fire to be found.

> Then he sent a little gray bird to the spirit world
> To bring from the campfires of the unseen country
> One living coal with which to make a fire
> For the cooking kettles and light-signals,
> And to warm the lodges of all the tribes
> That would follow him in suns to come.
>
> So the dauntless little gray bird
> Slowly winged across the far spaces.
> Three suns arose and set, and at the red evening
> When the third sun plunged its face in the sea,
> With all of its plumage burned a flame-tongue red,
> With a beak of red like hot coals
> And its face blackened with fire,
> Came the brave panting bird
> With a living coal held fast in its mouth,
> A coal snatched from the high altars
> Of the far country of the spirits.
>
> And so the fire gift was brought back to earth
> To warm the hearts and the wigwams
> Of every nation, for all seasons to come.[29]

Mrs. Porter was not above engaging in some real "huckstering" to promote the success of *The Firebird;* she wrote to a friend, "I want you to constitute yourself an amateur book agent and see what you can do for the sale of this volume among your friends, because the making of it has been so very expensive that, if it does not sell well, I never shall be permitted to make another."And later on in the same letter she says, "I am asking the people who love me and who have cared for what I have done formerly, to enlist with me in this battle, and to do whatever lies in their power to help me."[30] The effort must have been at least somewhat successful; Porter was allowed to produce one more book of poetry.

In spite of her real interest in Indians and her loathing of the depictions of Indian ways and customs which were only representative of the way writers thought Indians ought to have lived and in spite of her own striving for authenticity in her delineation—the same painstaking care evidenced in *Moths of the Limberlost*—she seems to have had little concern for the plight of the Indians. There is no record of her having spoken with her pen in behalf of the Indian nations who were suffering pitiable privation in the early years of the century.

Euphorbia is the only major work of Gene Stratton Porter which was serialized in a magazine but which did not achieve book status. The poem appeared serially in three issues of *Good Housekeeping*, January through March of 1923. According to Meehan it was the first poem so published, and Porter was paid more for it than any other poet had been paid for a poem.[31] There is little doubt that, had Porter lived, this opus would also have appeared between book covers. *Good Housekeeping* displayed the poem lavishly, with numerous illustrations by Dean Cornwell and began the first installment with a full-page portrait by James Montgomery Flagg bearing the caption, "Gene Stratton-Porter, whose name on the title pages of nearly ten million books entitles her to be called The Most Popular Woman Writer in the World."

Euphorbia tells the story of Marge Travers and her dissolute husband, Jacob, and of their successive failures. Never satisfied, Jacob drags his wife from Maine to the vineyards of New York, to the oil fields of Pennsylvania, to farms in Ohio and Kansas, to a cotton ranch in Arizona, and finally to California. Along the way, Marge bears and loses nine babies. Although Jacob sells the cotton ranch at a real profit, he is unable to afford the land by the sea they both so covet and is forced to settle for waste land at the edge of the desert. It is rich soil, there is water for irrigation, and incredibly hard work will make the land productive.

Love between the couple has long since died, and Jacob

develops an unrelenting hatred for Marge. He takes to drink and does all in his power to discomfort her. She becomes entranced by the beauty of desert plants and surreptitiously moves them to the yard of her house. Jacob, not in the least surreptitiously, sets about destroying them. Marge has a particular favorite, the *Euphorbia* of the title, which thrives at her doorstep. She saves it alone from Jacob's destructive rage by telling him that it is medicinal—that its pounded leaves and stems are a sure cure for rattlesnake and tarantula bites. In a fit of anger, Jacob tears up the plant and throws it far into the desert. Unsurprisingly, he suffers (or so he supposes) the strike of a rattler, and the precious plant is not at hand to save him. Actually, there is no snake; he dies of too much "white mule" (as Porter puts it) and too much hot desert sunshine, a combination which obviously is not compatible.

The last third of the poem is devoted to the redemption of Marge. She finds more money than she had expected in Jacob's money belt and refurbishes her house. She finds herself pregnant and successfully delivers her tenth child. She achieves the joys of permanence and motherhood. The *Euphorbia* grows again from its roots and spreads at her doorstep. In spite of her content, Marge lives in dread of discovering in Jacob, Junior, those traits of his father which made her life so intolerable. The fear becomes symbolized in the *Euphorbia*. When he is near two, Junior squats over it; Marge is terror stricken that he will destroy it, but he only pats it and calls it a pretty flower.

Porter claimed that *Euphorbia* was poetry, yet, confident as she was, she had some doubts:

. . . My eldest sister said . . . "It's a heart-breaking story. It flows the smoothest of anything I ever read in print; but for God's sake don't publish that and call it poetry!"

To me *Euphorbia* is poetry because it is written in the old ten- to eleven-syllable Miltonic verse form; because underlying it are the diffused rhythms of the outdoors as my ear picks them up on the highway, on the desert, in the mountains, in the meadows, in the open places. A few time it sweeps into the measures of the sea or the canyons. I said in speaking concerning it before the Poetry Society that I very gravely doubted whether I was entitled to call it poetry; I thought probably I should have called it a prose etching.[32]

Note that Porter had said almost the same thing of the rhythms

of *The Firebird.* However, she called *Euphorbia* blank verse
while she called *The Firebird* free verse. A sample will show that
the same flaws which mar the former are also present in the
latter, but also discernible are her genuine descriptive and
narrative powers:

> There came at last a memorable morning,
> When the tired horses were unable to climb farther,
> On which the weary road changed suddenly.
> It began to wind down colorful mountains;
> It crossed cool, alluring valleys
> And crept through crisp flower-bedecked canyons,
> Companioned by gaily-singing cold water,
>
> Then signs of civilization blended;
> Cultivated patches like gay carpets
> In delicate, green-veiled pastel colors,
> Spread on the sides of the maroon mountains;
>
> Little fields of anemic, discouraged corn,
> Squat adobe lodges of terra cotta,
> The flat roofs gold with drying husked corn,
> The walls festooned with strings of red peppers.
> Indians, wearing the trousers of today
> And the flaming head-band of the wild
> Passed them on the way to the rocky fields,
> Or, with well-filled quiver and shining bow,
> Going to the chase as their grandfathers,
> Because of the price of ammunition.[33]

Gene Stratton Porter's third major poetical work was *Jesus of
the Emerald.* In the research she engaged in for *Birds of the
Bible,* she had come across a legend concerning a portrait of the
Christ which had been carved by order of Tiberius Caesar on the
face of an emerald. This legend she turned into a poem.

The poem itself is not long, only three hundred lines or so, and
it takes up the first fifteen pages of the book. A nineteen-page
afterword is devoted to the Lentulus Legend on which the poem
is based and to Porter's investigation of the historical background. But again her publishers outdid themselves in the
production of a beautiful book. It was the time when "gift" books
were still popular at Christmas, and this book seems almost
specifically designed for a holiday remembrance. It was bound in

white boards with gilt decoration and a medallion of the Jesus portrait. It was boxed. The text was blocked in approximately twenty-line segments on double pages with wide margins embellished with color drawings by Edward Everett Winchell. It must have been as Porter claimed of the publication of *The Firebird*, "almost recklessly costly" to produce.[34]

The legend tells that one Publius Lentulus came before Tiberius Caesar and reported on the life and miracles of Jesus of Nazareth. Caesar sent a master-artist to study and observe the man and to record his picture. Tiberius was so awed by this likeness that he commanded the artist to choose from among the emperor's jewels the most suitable and engrave upon it the same likeness he had drawn; thus it might escape the ravages of time and preserve an authentic image of the Christ. The poem in its retelling of the legend pays particular attention to the selection of the emerald to bear the likeness and to the rejection of other stones. The artist chooses among alabaster (signifying purity), topaz (richness), sapphire (truth or joy), ruby (worldliness), and finally selects the emerald as a symbol of life and eternal renewal. The passage dealing with the contemplation of the topaz and its rejection is a fair sampling of the entire poem.

> Meditatively he touched the gold topaz.
> It seemed that the yellow lilies of the field
> Were deeply mirrored in its clear remoteness.
> He saw the faithful, amber-feathered hoopoe
> Winging life to his walled-in mate and nestlings,
> And heard the golden plover drumming love notes
> On each thickly wooded hill of Tuscany.
> In this jewel's depths he visioned the orange fruit
> And all the creeping gold of lavish nature.
> He saw the treasure of molten sun-like wealth,
> Deeply buried in the pulsing heart of earth;
> The life giving rays of the light of the world
> Jealously held fast in its shining compass.
> But he could not feel the symbol of riches
> To be the stone that his moved heart demanded
> On which to set forever the God-like face.[35]

The poem is written in the same "Miltonic blank verse" as is *Euphorbia*. It seems as if Porter had consciously striven to achieve eleven syllabled lines, resulting in roughly truncated hexameters yielding a strained rather than a pleasing cadence.

The images and pictures that she employs in her overall construct are from her beloved nature; from birds, as witness the hoopoe and the plover; and from plants, the yellow lilies, the orange fruit, and "all the creeping gold of lavish nature." This tendency to draw from nature is recognized throughout the poem, but it lacks the authenticity of the work in the real nature books. Porter had not the familiarity with the Holy Land or with Italy which she had with the central United States or even with California and which made her natural history observations ring true. In regard to the passage quoted above, "yellow lilies of the field," most authorities agree that the biblical lilies of the field were most likely *Anemone coronaria,* and yellow is a color not to be found in this grouping. Such a questionable usage Porter would never have been guilty of in writing of plants familiar to her.

There is yet another major poem by Gene Stratton Porter. This is the lengthy, 350-line poem *Whitmore's Bull,* which appeared in the June 1926 issue of *McCall's.* It is a narrative related by a little girl telling the story of an escaped bull and its determination to feed on the lushness of her mother's garden and of her father's prowess and equal determination that it should not so feed. Her father in this poem is not the Mark Stratton depicted in other writings, but a younger, more virile man:

> Father was not large, but he was large enough.
> His forhead was high, his mouth wide,
> His eyes a steady steel-blue in color.
> His hair was fine, dark and slightly wavy,
> The contour of his face was sharply chisled,
> While on his high defiant cheek bones
> There burned always the unfading flush
> Of roast-beef red of old England.
> His legs were firm as the arch support to a bridge.
> His back was broad like Atlas in the mythology book,
> Big skeins of living whipcord were his muscles.
> He was a beautiful figure of virile manhood.

The story is a simple one, but it is told with all the genius for storytelling that Porter possessed to a superlative degree. The bull escapes from its pasture, wanders down the road, is attacked by a watch dog, stung by aroused yellow-jackets, and—

infuriated—arrives at the garden where the storyteller and her father are busily repairing a picket fence around the mother's beloved garden. The father gives it a benumbing tap—not a blow—on a strategic spot below the ear and drives it home by twisting its tail. That is all, and yet the reader is carried along by the sheer interestingness of the storytelling. Not only are the characters of little girl, father, and bull sharply drawn, but the setting, a glorious May day in rural Indiana, is carefully depicted. The action, and there is action aplenty, is intense and straightforward. There is never a doubt as to which is to be the winner in the contest between man and bull.

> To our wood-yard gate Father followed the bull,
> At every step administering punishment,
> While at each twist the big creature bellowed loudly
> And gathered momentum as he proceeded.

The poem ends with the exultant triumph of the man, the complete abjection of the bull, and the somewhat philosophic reflection of the little girl.

> He [Father] was laughing and breathing in short gusts
> When he came back to where I was standing,
> Picked up his saw, and went on pointing the pickets.
> "I'll wager a pretty His Imperial Majesty
> Comes not this way again in many a day," he said.
>
> Silently I gazed at my Father,
> Then I looked up the pink and white walled road
> Hourly beckoning to each seeker of conquests,
> And watched the bull turning Steele's corner.
> He was traveling at a wabbling drag-trot,
> Hugging the fence closely for protection,
> Still of threatening voice, raising no dust,
> His dry tongue hanging from his mouth,
> While his huge head seemed as if it were so heavy
> That never again could he exultantly lift it.
> Sick, dirt-encrusted, beaten and abject,
> He was hurrying to the safety of his meadow.
>
> I sat down on a stack of pickets, until I was needed,
> And thought deeply about my Father;
> Then I thought even longer about Whitmore's bull.[36]

This poem was, supposedly, the last to be written by Gene Stratton Porter, and it certainly deserves consideration as her best; it is forcefully entertaining, highly descriptive, and almost entirely devoid of sentimentality. Structurally it comes near to escaping the faults that mar her other poetic works—the lines for the most part run smoothly, and the rhythms are fast-moving, natural, and exciting. If Gene Stratton Porter deserves recognition as a poet, her reputation might well rest on *Whitmore's Bull*. And yet it is forgotten. It was never reprinted from *McCall's*, no anthology boasts of it, and no mention of it is made in the writing of Porter, Meehan, or other authorities on this life.

According to her own account, Gene Stratton Porter was encouraged to continue her work with poetry and received high commendation from Charles Wharton Stork, William Sloan Kennedy, and others of lesser note. However, one can only wonder if Dr. Stork, editor of *Contemporary Verse*, who never printed any of Mrs. Porter's poems, was not playing with her when he wrote in response to her query as to whether or not she could write poetry, "My dear lady, you have never written anything else,"[37] and, "You are a poet just as truly as you are a novelist,"[38] and finally, "I believe your epics will live longer than your novels." But, in all fairness, one must add the remainder of the quotation, "and will fall into place with the best we have done thus far in this country."[39]

In several places Gene Stratton Porter tells of having destroyed much of her early poetic work and of having regretted doing so. "When I sacrificed my first three efforts at poetry, I was the victim of some extremely ill-advised advice from a person upon whose judgment I had the misfortune to rely utterly." And there is a curious reference which may or may not be to a long poem never published. "I have wasted a thousand things as fine as 'The Wine Pitcher' in the past twenty years because I thought they were no good, and I would not take the time from the work I knew I could do, that would be appreciated by people in general, to write the visions that came to me; and when I did write anything, for the greater part it met the fate of 'The Wine Pitcher' which is still awaiting its day after nearly twenty years."[40] If such a poem ever was written, it seems to be no longer in existence.

The poetry of Gene Stratton Porter, while mostly of great length, is never of a sustained effort. It is true that there are many poetic lines, indeed many poetic passages, but the quality of the writing too often fails to measure up to the quality of the plan. She considered her poetry to be a far better thing than her novels and on a par with or superior to her nature books. But, unless there is a great change in the appraisal of the popular culture of the first quarter of the twentieth century, Porter's place in the history of that culture in that period must be established by her fiction and by her natural history—not by her poems.

Gene Stratton Porter was aware of the poetic revolution that peaked in the decade of 1910-20 and which had its greatest expression in *The New Poetry*, edited by Harriet Monroe and Alice Corbin Henderson, and in *Poetry, A Magazine of Verse* edited by Monroe. She subscribed to *Poetry* and was acquainted (at least by correspondence) with Harriet Monroe. Porter suggested that she contribute to *Poetry*, but there is no record of a response by Harriet Monroe.

V   *Photographer and Illustrator*

There were several activities which accompanied or grew out of the writing career of Gene Stratton Porter. As has been suggested, photography was the impetus which gave rise to the writing in the first place. It is useless to conjecture what might have happened had she not become interested in the camera. And yet her earliest work was not illustrated with her own photographs, nor were any of the novels after *The Song of the Cardinal.* But photography is so closely interwoven with writing in the nature articles and books that it is impossible to separate the careers. The same thing is true of her work as an illustrator; her drawings and colored photographs were done with but one purpose—to enhance the beauty of her books. In like manner, she became a producer of motion pictures solely to bring her fiction before the *viewing* public with as much fidelity to the original text and the moral intent as was possible. There were other activities which stemmed from the main career. She contributed to publications dealing with birds or with photography. She wrote books for children. She was interested in the stage and with adaptations of her work to be presented dramatically.

Photography around the turn of the century was still an

emerging medium. For the most part, Gene Stratton Porter worked with cameras whose exposures were made on glass plates. It was a slow and intricate process. While snapshots were not unknown, the best results required time exposures from a set camera. Such work involved Mrs. Porter's locating the nest, setting and focusing the camera, concealing it, and then familiarizing herself with the birds so that they paid little or no attention to her or to the camera and behaved naturally. And she drew on the experiences of her girlhood on Hopewell Farm.

My first feeling on going afield was one of amazement at what my early days among the birds had taught me. Then I was merely amusing myself, following inborn tendencies. Now I learned with every approach to the home of a bird that I was using knowledge acquired in childhood. I knew what location each bird would choose for her nest, how she would build it, brood, and care for her young. When I wanted the picture of any particular bird I knew exactly where to search for its nest, so no time was wasted. When I found a nest, all that was necessary was to set up a camera before it, focus it sharply, cover the camera to the lens with a green cloth or a few twigs, then repeat the methods of childhood. The birds had not changed in the slightest; nor had I. By using tact, patience, and plain common sense, and drawing on former experience, in three days or less I was on a working basis with any nest of birds I ever attempted to cultivate, so that I could secure poses of the old birds performing every action of their lives anywhere in the locality of their nests.

I have reproduced birds in fear, anger, greed, pride, surprise, in full tide of song, while dressing the plumage, taking a sun bath, courting, brooding, and carrying food to their young. My procedure was merely to turn child's play into woman's work. My methods must be followed by any one who desires to accustom wild creatures to a state of fellowship with humanity. In order to do this, it is necessary to move slowly, to live among the birds until one thoroughly understands their characteristics and habits, to remain near their location until they have become accustomed to one as a part of their daily life that they will be perfectly natural in one's presence.[41]

It seems at first indeed unfortunate that Gene Stratton Porter did not live in the era of modern photography—especially color photography. But on the other hand, lacking the necessity for limitless patience and perfect empathy with the birds imposed upon her by her equipment, the superb natural photographs she secured might not have come about. Nature photographers now are legion, and there are constantly appearing artistic and accurate studies of bird life. Yet the photographs of birds taken by Gene Stratton Porter three quarters of a century ago can and do hold their place with the best of them. As recently as summer 1976, an exhibit of her work at Ball State University drew thousands of visitors who were not only able to view and to judge the nature studies of Porter, but could compare them with contemporary prints displayed in adjoining galleries.[42]

It is quite safe to assume that the pioneer work of Porter in portraying birds was a great influence on her contemporaries and on photographers who were to follow her. To a greater or lesser extent, the method she developed and explained through her writing had to be followed if utterly natural pictures were to be secured.

One unanswered question is, what became of the negatives and plates Gene Stratton Porter exposed? In *Homing with the Birds* she says, "There are hundreds of negatives in my closet,"[43] and "among my plates now numbering thousands,"[44] but with the exception of the pictures which were used to illustrate books and magazine articles, few seem to be extant. A letter from her grandson John E. Meehan to Anastasia Clothier Hathaway written in 1974 states that "to the best of our knowledge . . . none of the plates . . . are in existence." It seems that except for a few miscellaneous pictures and the illustrations which were published, Porter's extensive photographic output has perished.

Mrs. Porter was always interested in the appearance of her books, and she planned her volumes—expecially the nature books—from cover to cover. She used her considerable talents as a water colorist and as an illustrator in the production of these books. If she did not feel capable of producing the drawings she wanted to use with sufficient dexterity, she sent rough sketches of her desires to her publishers to be done professionally, but always the finished product had to meet with her approval. *The Song of the Cardinal* (in the first edition) was her work from beginning to end, even to the colored plate used as a frontispiece. To secure this picture Mrs. Porter used the same technique she was to employ later so successfully in *Moths of the Limberlost*. Using a special print-paper which provided at the same time a distinct but faint photographic image and a surface capable of taking water color pigment, she overlaid color on the print with meticulous attention to detail. In all her nature books she maintained the same vigorous and active control of the book making exactly as she wanted it, and her publishers yielded to her demands. After all, Gene Stratton Porter was one of the most lucrative possessions a publishing house could have.

VI *Motion Picture Producer*

The final career that grew out of the life of Gene Stratton Porter was that of motion picture producer. The great upsurge in the production of moving pictures in America came after World War I. The economic boom of the 1920s, coupled with the flush of victory, transformed the America of the early years of the century, when idealism and romanticism still flourished, into a land of moral uncertainty and laxity such as the country had never before experienced. The violent reversals in manners and morals occasioned by the ending of the war were reflected in the moving pictures of the time. There is neither space nor the inclination to chronicle here the corruption that invaded the movie industry in the 1920s.

All through the jazz decade there was an undercurrent of protest against the licentiousness of the period. Much of the protest was unorganized and futile. But church and school groups and women's clubs were both vocal and effective. Porter believed that the same wholesome virtues of goodness and morality that permeated her novels would make them vehicles to bring back goodness and morality into American life if they were translated to the medium of the silver screen. But, although movie producers were anxious to tap the enormous popular audience of Mrs. Porter, they wanted to make their pictures of her novels in their own way. Strong-willed and determined as she was, she would have no part of that—her novels must be reproduced faithfully on the screen or not at all. She had had one unfortunate experience; one of her early books had been made into a movie much to her disgust.[45] Meehan writes of this occurrence:

Since her arrival in California Mother had been besieged by various picture companies to sell them the picture rights to her books. At first she was not particularly interested, and refused them all point blank without even an interview because of one unfortunate experience. She had allowed a well-known company to do one of her early books. They had invited her to approve the adaptation and continuity and make suggestions; all of which she did. But when they made the picture, they ignored all of her ideas and suggestions. Consequently, the result was very unsatisfactory and disappointing to Mother, and she declared that no more pictures would be made until she was ready to make them herself.[46]

And make them she did. She was a wealthy woman from the royalties on her books which were selling in unprecedented numbers. While her popularity as evidenced by the sales of her later books may have been somewhat diminished, *Michael O'Halloran* in 1916 having been the last of her top best-sellers, *The White Flag* (1923) achieved the highest prepublication sales of any book in American publishing history to date, and the voice of "Gene Stratton-Porter's Page" appeared monthly in McCall's, reaching and influencing millions of faithful readers. She had the necessary money; therefore, she organized Gene Stratton-Porter Productions and went into the business. She fought the same fight she had fought with her publishers to get the pictures which she kept true to the books as she conceived them before the viewing public. She had no fight as far as production was concerned—she owned the company, and her daughter, Jeannette, was married to her director, James Leo Meehan, so it was pretty much a family affair. The struggle was to convince booking organizations and exhibitors that the pictures would be accepted by audiences with the "nature stuff" and the emphasis on decency left in. As usual, she won; and, as usual, she was right—her loyal readership was perfectly willing to follow her into the moving picture theater.

During her lifetime four of the novels became movies produced by her own company: *Michael O'Halloran, A Girl of the Limberlost, Laddie,* and *The Keeper of the Bees;* although the last named was not released until after her death, she was active in the major stages of its production. After her death, *The Magic Garden, The Harvester,* and *Freckles* were produced under the banner of Gene Stratton-Porter Productions. The outdoor scenes for *The Harvester* were filmed in Indiana at Wildflower Woods in 1927.[47] Gene Stratton Porter movies continued to be produced and continued to be popular. A total of some twenty Porter films

were released between 1917 and 1960, including three presenta-
tions of *Freckles*.[48]

Gene Stratton Porter was quick to utilize the forces gathering
against corruption in the movies and to turn at least a part of the
tide in favor of her own pictures. She had a great deal of
influence with the Women's Clubs of the Los Angeles area and
with the State and National Federations. She was adamant
against "indecent pictures, indecent books, and indecent dances"
and urged clubwomen all over the country to take a firm stand
against these evils. She appeared frequently on the lecture
platform at club conventions and at other gatherings and she
wrote numerous letters enlisting the support of women all over
the country for the movement she was so interested in. In August
of 1925 (after her death) there appeared an advertisement in
McCall's asking viewers to request FBO (Film Booking Office of
America) to show the movie *Keeper of the Bees*. A coupon was
attached which readers could fill out and return to FBO. The
advertisement stressed the cleanliness and wholesomeness of the
film and promised that "next month's ad will give the cast." It
did, and interestingly enough, the Little Scout was played by
Mrs. Porter's granddaughter, and the part of Lolly was played by
Clara Bow.

An evidence of the modernity of Gene Stratton Porter appears
in the ease with which what she believed about children and
motion pictures can be compared with prevalent attitudes
toward television and children. She saw the error of believing
that all motion pictures should be made so that children might
see them.

. . . This is a mistaken idea. There are books for children, pictures for
children, magazines for children, and there is music for children. You
do not expect to allow your child to read *all* the books in your libraries,
nor to understand *all* the music he hears, nor to attend *all* legitimate
theatrical productions. Then why insist that you will be able to take him
to *all* moving pictures? There will be many not suitable for children,
just as there will be books, music, plays, and magazines not suitable for
children. Why insult the intelligence of a moving-picture audience by
making all pictures suitable for children?

Parents must have some control over what "movies" their children
attend, just as they supervise their other forms of education and

entertainment. There are many pictures made which are entirely proper for children, and children should be restricted to those pictures. I should not like to believe that every time I went to see a moving picture I was going to see one made for a child; for I think I am capable of understanding and appreciating an entertainment that a child is not. I do not believe any adult entertainment should be so limited to the comprehension of a child, nor to that degree of intimate problems suited to childish minds and morals.[49]

There is little doubt that Gene Stratton Porter was one of the major influences which forced upon Hollywood the self-imposed censorship of the Hays Office. This, then, was the accomplishment of Porter as movie producer. Had she lived, it surely would have been much more. She financed and produced the film versions of her own books—just as she wanted them—and she lent the influence of her pen and her person to the movement for decency and morality in the film industry as a whole.

VII *Curiosity and Ephemera*

Gene Stratton Porter wrote four books which do not fit into the classifications of novels, nature books, or poetry. Two of them are children's books, one is a *Programme* written especially for a whistler, and one is a collection of essays.

After the Flood is a collection of children's stories. The flood is Noah's flood, and the book deals with various experiences of the animals and birds in adjusting to the new life, or in one case failing to adjust because of bitter experience on the Ark. The stories are told in a Hoosier dialect which at best is a poor imitation of James Whitcomb Riley. The book is full of foolish puns such as, "Dr. Wood Duck, a notorious quack," and abounds throughout in attempts to be humorous. True to her life-long love affair with cardinals, the opening story is about how the cardinal got his red coat. The Indian legend of *The Fire Bird* was to come later; this account is that of a bird who was so inquisitive and bothersome while Mother Nature was painting things anew after the flood that she dipped him in red paint. Another story explains the raucous "laughter" of loons as being due to the fact that the loons were water birds and there was no water in the Ark for them to swim and disport themselves, with the result that they went crazy.

This book, which was printed by Bobbs-Merrill for—and perhaps commissioned by—the Indiana Society of Chicago, is an example of Gene Stratton Porter's use and reuse of her material. Perhaps the Indiana Society, intent on putting out a collection of the work of selected Indiana authors, requested that Mrs. Porter contribute one volume. Perhaps she gathered together some stories she was writing for a planned children's book and submitted them. There is no way of knowing. But of the five titles in *After the Flood*, four appear intact in *Morning Face*, and the loon story is also in *Birds of the Limberlost*.

Morning Face was written for and about Gene Stratton Porter's little granddaughter, Gene. It is a collection of the stories a doting grandmother with a propensity for nature might spin for the child and of the verses she might make up to pass away idle hours. Neither the stories nor the poems have literary merit, but they do possess a certain charm. Much of this charm exudes from the gentle humor which pervades the book, and humor was not one of the qualities dominating the children's literature of the first quarter of the twentieth century. Parents might have found this book helpful in the rearing of their own offspring, for hardly concealed within the stories and verses were Mrs. Porter's methods for teaching nature study to the very young. Moreover, there were suggested many activities which parents could encourage their children to follow which would enable them to enjoy the natural world around them.

Gene Stratton Porter's publishers were generous with her in the publication of her nonfiction. Knowing that the books could not be expected to show more than a modest profit, they allowed her the use of expensive papers, artwork, and binding; in addition, they permitted a profligate use of her own photographs—*Morning Face* has eighty pictures in black and white and one in color. The result is that *Morning Face* (along with *Moths of the Limberlost*) is one of the most attractive of Porter's books to own. It is also one of the rarest and most expensive.[50] While her publishers would pamper Mrs. Porter with the fine books she wanted, they would not issue large editions. There were only two American and one English printings of *Morning Face*, as contrasted with the forty-three English-language printings of *Laddie* and the twenty-nine editions of *A Girl of the Limberlost*.

Most curious of all of the publications of Gene Stratton Porter and the one which best illustrates the power she held over her publishers is *Birds of the Limberlost*. It is also a disappointment to one who knows *Moths of the Limberlost*, and expects to find here a companion volume similar in scope and in execution. Scarcely worth being called a book, it consists of twenty-four pages bound in a stiff paper cover. It is a "programme especially prepared for Katharine Minahan." Now, Katharine Minahan was a socialite soprano who, because of the peculiar structure of her throat, was able to imitate bird calls with an amazing accuracy.[51] Whether Gene Stratton Porter prepared the program at Miss Minahan's request or whether she simply thought it would be appropriate for her is not known, nor has any record of the program ever having been performed been discovered. But Doubleday, Page & Company dutifully published it. An examination of the parts of this program reveals that it was all selected from *After the Flood* or from *Morning Face. After the Flood* was issued in 1911. *Birds of the Limberlost* was printed in 1914, while *Morning Face* did not come until 1916. Evidently the materials were at hand, and the program was put together from these sources.

Birds of the Limberlost would be of even less consequence than it is if it were not for the incidents in *Michael O'Halloran* in which much is made of Malcolm Minturn's learning to imitate birds and of his mother's having done the same to the extent that they end up calling each other (as birds) and a happy reunion results. There is a lesser but recurring theme of Mrs. Porter's— that not only can humans learn to imitate birds to the extent of enticing them, but that birds have also contributed much to the composers of music. For not only in *Michael O'Halloran,* but also in *Freckles,* in *A Girl of the Limberlost* and in *The Harvester* is this relationship expressed, but it is a large part, as the title would suggest, of *Music of the Wild.*

Let Us Highly Resolve, the posthumous volume of essays by Gene Stratton Porter, requires little attention. The essays were mostly ones which were written for and had appeared in *McCall's.* That some are different or bear different titles would indicate that some of the originals were revised or rewritten, but for all practical purposes they are a selection from the articles which appeared over a six-year span as "Gene Stratton-Porter's Page" in the monthly issues of the magazine.

Two other writing activities of Porter's are worthy of note. As

a result of her writing *Birds of the Bible* she was asked to do the
bird articles for the *International Bible Encyclopedia.* In a
response to one of her critics she cites this assignment as proof of
the veracity of her bird studies, ". . .which leaves my natural
history of a brand acceptable to the doctors of science compiling
the Encyclopedia I mentioned—and they had the ornithologists
of the world from which to make a choice to do the work."[52] No
doubt this work was quite time consuming, but it seems to have
been motivated by a real interest in the subject and not from a
want for money.

The last piece of ephemera worthy of recognition is the
contribution she made to the *Photographic Times Almanac* for
1902. An article entitled "From the Viewpoint of a Field
Worker" tells how she worked in much the same manner as it
was told in magazine articles and in her books and is illustrated
with a dozen or so of her photographs many of which appeared
again in later publications. It is only the early date of this article
(the *Almanac* was published in 1901) which makes it notewor-
thy.[53]

CHAPTER 3

The Books of Fiction

I   Getting Started

G ENE Stratton Porter's first novel, *The Song of the Cardinal*, was published in 1903. It grew out of the indignation she felt at having found the body of a cardinal wantonly shot by a hunter to prove his marksmanship. It was first written as a short story and submitted to *Century Magazine*. The editor, Richard Watson Gilder, saw that it had book possibilities and suggested that she expand the story and submit it with his recommendation to Bobbs-Merrill, the publishing firm in her own state. This she did, the manuscript was accepted, and the career that touched so many lives was fully under way.

The Song of the Cardinal has little literary merit. The two plots—bird and human—are disparate and the scenes too much separated. The birds are given human characteristics and human emotions, and sentimentality is rife. Yet the book does have a certain charm, and after all Aesop and countless other fabulists have been appealing to people for ages. In present times, what about *Watership Down* and *Jonathan Livingston Seagull?* The fact is that there was an audience waiting for such a book, and it was an extensive audience.

The story is simply the life story of a red bird and his mate coupled with the story of a farmer and his wife whose lives are enriched by their association with the birds. The character Abram in the book is modeled upon the author's father, Mark Stratton. The main flaw in the book is the interminably long uninterrupted homily delivered against the hunter who strays on to Abram's land. Perhaps one should remember that Mark Stratton was a country preacher and that his daughter may have been recalling interminably long sermons in the little church in the Hopewell community.

Gene Stratton Porter never considered *The Song of the Cardinal* a novel but claimed it as a nature book. But she was a shrewd business woman; she realized that the market of the time called for fiction, not nature books. She knew that she could tell a story, and she knew that through setting, scene, and incident she could work in the nature which was so dear to her. And so she produced *Freckles*.

Doubleday, Page & Company, who were to become her main publishers, accepted *Freckles* even though they were convinced that it would not sell unless much of the "nature stuff" were eliminated. But Porter refused:

From the start I realized that I never could reach the audience I wanted with a book on nature alone. To spend time writing a book based wholly on human passion and its outworking, I would not. So I compromised on a book into which I put all the nature work that came naturally within its scope, and seasoned it with little bits of imagination and straight copying from the lives of men and women I had known intimately, folk who lived in a simple, common way and with which I was familiar. So I said to my publishers; "I will write the books exactly as they take shape in my mind. You publish them. I know they will sell enough that you will not lose. If I do not make $600 on a book, I shall never utter a complaint. Make up my work as I think it should be and leave it to the people as to what kind of book they will take into their hearts and homes."[1]

Porter won her battle and the "nature stuff" stayed in. There is little doubt that she was right. Without the rich background of nature lore which pervades all the novels, with the possible exception of *The White Flag*, Porter would be only another of the many ephemeral popular novelists of the early years of the century. It is only the author's deep love of the natural world around her and her ability to transmit this love to others which gives her work any permanence—this and her indisputable ability to tell a story.

Her second novel (or perhaps her first by her count), *Freckles*, is the story of a homeless stray who wanders into a lumber camp in the Limberlost and becomes a guard for a valuable tract of timber. His first task is to overcome his fear of the swamp region. He meets the Swamp Angel and the Bird Woman (Porter herself) and has numerous adventures with both the swamp and with timber thieves. He wins the love and respect of John McLean, the timber boss, to the extent that he becomes his foster son. Freckles thwarts the timber thieves and wins the Swamp Angel, but he must determine his own identity to be worthy of her. This task is accomplished almost too handily with the help of the Angel, and Freckles becomes, in fact, Lord Terrence O'More.

The plot is timeworn—the lost waif who finds his name—and the story is highly sentimental and romantic. But it is also swift-moving and adventuresome. Perhaps nowhere in all her writing did Porter excel in the usage of nature as background for story as she employs it in Freckles. The reader willingly suspends his disbelief for, as one reviewer put it, "It is a very pleasing story, the unreality of which has nothing to do with the case. In the forests of Arden one does not bother with brute possibilities, nor does one or need one in the Limberlost Swamp, where also the world is younger and kinder than most people find it outside of enchanted places."[2]

An interesting point concerning *Freckles* is that the story of its publication reveals Gene Stratton Porter as more of an artist than she is usually given credit for being. Her original title for the book was *The Falling Feather,* and its impact was tragic. The book ended where the falling tree crushed Freckles, presumably killing him. Considered from this viewpoint the story—much shortened—has an artistic unity and lacks much of the contrivance and cloying sentimentality of the published version. But the time was not right for such a story with almost Hawthornian implications. The great reading public demanded its happy ending.

Three separate publishing houses read and rejected this original manuscript, but each saw merit in the book and would publish it with the expanded happy ending and with the emphasis on nature greatly reduced or omitted altogether.

Porter was dissatisfied, but

. . . I gave in, and I wish now that I had not; but at the time I thought I was forced, and I rather think so still. I had no audience and no funds to publish and exploit my own work. If I would not conform sufficiently to the judgment of the publishers so that they would bring out my books I could reach the people with no part of my message, and a lifetime of work spent in equipping myself for the work I was eager to do would be wasted to all save myself. The true flavour of the book was spoiled for me; but many have liked it as it stands. . . .

However, Gene Stratton Porter was adamant as to the retention of the nature writing:

Each publisher who saw it before production assured me that the nature stuff it contained would kill any chance it might otherwise have of becoming a popular book, and felt sure that if I would cut that out, it would bring me fame and money. I replied that the sole purpose of the book was to put the nature stuff it contained before the people. I had no desire for fame, or more than a very plain living; if I changed the title and amplified the text that was all the concession I could possibly make.[3]

Eventually there was a compromise, and the artistically faulted but nature-entire *Freckles* was published. That it reached millions of readers is well established. But one wonders what might have been the fate of *The Falling Feather* and what might have happened to later books if Gene Stratton Porter had not forced herself to accept the formula for popularity to assure a readership for her nature studies. As she concludes, "I still mourn for my little classic that might have been."

In 1907, *At the Foot of the Rainbow* was published. This book is one of the best-constructed of the novels. The conflict is well established, and there is a unity—a singleness of purpose—which other books lack. It is a Wabash River rather than a Limberlost book, although it is of the Wabash in the vicinity of the Limberlost rather than the Wabash of her childhood, and it deals with the activities of two men trapping and fishing in that region. Its plot, stated baldly, is the most sensational of all Porter's works and could well deny the charge that her fiction was all sugar and molasses. It is the story of three people, a man in love with both a husband and a wife. Such stories were not written—at least not for popular audiences—in the early 1900s, and the publisher's synopsis puts it, "Central Indiana furnishes the rural scene of a story whose characters—two men and a woman—constitute the modern-drama triangle. It is a tale of a heroic Scotchman's friendship for a dissipated Irishman who had played the former false when entrusted with a message to the girl both loved."[4]

The story is interestingly told and there is more in-depth

characterization than is common to most Porter novels. The character of Mary Malone is quite sympathetically drawn, and she emerges as one of the most appealing of Porter's heroines. (That there is a remarkable resemblance between her and Marge Travers, the heroine of the long poem *Euphorbia*, is incidental, or coincidental.) Beyond its story, the book is worth reading because of the background of outdoor life, nature, and of the changing pageant of the seasons. This book is the only one written by Porter in which hunting, trapping, and fishing feature to any great extent. And it is conservation oriented; the two men lure wildlife to their holdings and post their land for the protection of birds and animals not in their own interest but as a refuge against hunters.

Meehan refers to the arrangement—whether tacit or contractual is not clear—to alternate nature novels which would be money makers with nature books which would not be as profitable. "Because the nature books alone scarcely paid expenses, she promised her publishers that she would alternate with first a nature book and then a novel. So, in December, 1907, she published *At the Foot of the Rainbow*, which contained the requisite romance and also a portion of natural history."[5] However, *At the Foot of the Rainbow* was published by the Outing Company and by Grosset and Dunlap in 1907. There is no edition bearing the Doubleday, Page logo until 1910. Also, *What I Have Done with Birds* was published in 1907 by Bobbs-Merrill. It would seem, then, that if there ever was such a formal arrangement with her publishers (Doubleday, Page) it must have come at a later date.

Freckles was slow in obtaining popularity, but *At the Foot of the Rainbow* added to the growing number of Porter readers, and the publication of *A Girl of the Limberlost* in 1909, which was billed as a sequel to *Freckles*, created an upsurge of interest in the earlier book which gave added impetus to its phenomenal sales record. Thus by 1909 Mrs. Porter had become an established author both as naturalist and novelist and her career as a writer was fully launched.

II   *Nature and Autobiography*

A Girl of the Limberlost is often called an autobiographical novel. It is so only in the sense that all of Gene Stratton Porter's books were drawn from her own life and experience. With this fact in mind it is apparent that Elnora Comstock as girl naturalist may mirror Gene Stratton Porter, but that Elnora as story heroine is purely imaginative. The happenings in the Limberlost were those of Porter herself, but the happenings in the novel were the fictitious attributions of the novelist to her heroine. This claim is supported by the intrusion of the writer in her own person as the Bird Woman into the story. This is Porter the naturalist befriending the imaginary girl who has similar experiences in the great swamp.

The story is simple. Elnora's mother, Kate Comstock, has never forgiven her daughter for the fact that Elnora's birth prevented her from saving her husband from the quagmire of the Limberlost. She grudgingly supports Elnora to the extent that the law demands, but Elnora is forced to secure her education in the local high school by selling the products of the swamp, mainly butterflies and moths, to the Bird Woman for her own collection and for exchange with collectors around the world. In spite of her own privations, she befriends Billy, the son of an alcoholic and profligate father who dies in a drunken stupor, and finds him a home with the Sintons, her neighbors and parent subrogates. A romance develops with Philip Ammon, a wealthy young Chicagoan recuperating in the neighborhood of the Limberlost from a serious illness; a romance complicated by the fact that Philip is already engaged to socialite Edith Carr. The rejuvenation and regeneration of Kate Comstock, the reformation of Billy, and the resolution of the romantic triangle take up the rest of the book. *A Girl of the Limberlost* is no doubt at the same time the shallowest yet one of the most enthralling of Porter's romances. It also reached a vast audience and, with *Freckles,* did much to quicken the interest of a large public in nature—in the outdoors and the plant and animal inhabitants thereof.

The Harvester in 1911 was another prod to middle-class America to get out into the open, to appreciate and to enjoy natural history. The Harvester, David Langston, lived in the woods and made his living by harvesting the medicinal seeds, roots, and herbs he found there. He sees the vision of a beautiful girl, and the rest of the book is devoted to his search for and ultimate winning of her through the overcoming of obstacles of poverty, illness, and pride. He also experiments with the curative powers of natural products and concocts a remedy which not only saves the life of the girl but wins him national recognition as an authority on natural medicines.

The Harvester, David Langston, was modeled in part on the character of Thoreau as Porter imagined him to be and in part on her memories of her father. Again, *The Harvester* exemplifies the main thesis of the influence of life upon writer. While David is *not* Gene Stratton Porter, the experiences he had in the woods, the attitude he had toward nature and mankind, and his general philosophic outlook are those of the author. The book is highly romantic and idealistic and, as the *New York Times* put it, "In spite of one or two glaring faults [it] is worthy of warm commendation because of its strong individual note, its sincerity, and especially because in its conception and its working out its aim is toward idealism. And the Lord of Novels knows how rare a quality that is in American fiction."[6]

In 1913 *Laddie* appeared. Here is autobiography pure and simple. The "novel" merely tells the story of Geneva Grace Stratton as a little girl. It is a faithful account of the life of her family on Hopewell Farm, and the members of her family are easily identified as the central characters in the book. Chiefly it is the story of her beloved brother, Leander, or Laddie as he is called in the book and of the romance with the Princess, the daughter of an aristocratic English father who for some reason or other has "lost" himself and his family in the backwoods of Indiana. The characters are all real and according to her own account:

I could write no truer biography. To the contour of hill and field, to the last stripe on the wall paper and knot on the door, that is the home in which I was born, the parents who reared me, the very words they said and the things they did, the exact circumstances of my birth, my brothers and sisters, and some of my friends. There was no such person as "Mrs. Freshett," and a few of the things told never really happened; but three-fourths of it is exact truth. If you will read "Stratton" for "Stanton," "Northbrooke" for "Eastbrooke" you will have the truth in the case as straight as I can tell it.[7]

It would not be Porter if it were not idealized, romanticized, and fictionalized more than a little bit, but then it would not be good reading either, and *Laddie* is perhaps the most readable of all Porter's books. Even today, it bears comparison with the best of the regionalists for one who wishes to recapture or to come to know a section of the land in a time long past.

A writing of Mrs. Porter's unfortunately unidentified and undated states: "People generally ask where Laddie is now and what became of the Princess. Laddie was drowned before his marriage to the Princess occurred. I saw her sit on her beautiful horse at the foot of his grave and watch the casket that contained the beautiful body lowered into the earth. In later years she married a man with whom all of us were acquainted. She retained her beauty and charm of manner well on to middle age, and died only a few years ago."[8]

At the end of the second "Laddie" story which Gene Stratton Porter sold to *Metropolitan Magazine* in 1901, there is this curious appendage which must have puzzled readers who naturally had not read the book which did not appear for twelve years and who were totally unacquainted with the story of Leander's drowning. "O Laddie! Laddie! I know you had to do it. You never could have seen a companion drown and not make an effort to save him. But when the cruel water shut the light from your dear eyes forever, it killed your mother, struck joy from the life of the Princess, and left forever an ache in the heart of your little sister."[9] This passage is doubly strange because the facts as reported in the *Wabash Plain Dealer* of July 18, 1872, report the exact opposite interpretation; it was Leander who was drowning and the companion who tried to save *him*.[10]

These, then, are the books that established Gene Stratton Porter as an author with an immense and loyal following; these are the books that best depict her native Indiana; and these are the books that are most revealing of the life of their creator. This is not to say that had her publication started in 1915 instead of 1903 she would not have achieved success. This is not to say that in subsequent books her life and her environment no longer played a part. This is not to say that after *Laddie,* her life vanished from her books. It is simply to say that in these three books, *The Harvester, A Girl of the Limberlost,* and *Laddie,* there is more of Porter's particular brand of nature writing and more revelation concerning her life than in any others.

In 1915, Gene Stratton Porter revised her books along lines suggested by her publishers, and new and revised editions of *The Song of the Cardinal, Freckles, At the Foot of the Rainbow, A Girl of the Limberlost, The Harvester,* and *Laddie* appeared.

Porter wrote, ". . .They now stand in the form I am willing to leave them."[11]

III   *The City and the Farm*

In 1915 came *Michael O'Halloran* with a new setting and a new theme, the debilitating effect of society on life. It is a city setting, and a double plot of "rags to riches" (triumph over adversity) and the re-creation of lives near ruined by wealth and arrogance. It is the story of Mickey, a quick-witted and determined Irish newsboy, who adopts a crippled waif, Lily Peaches, and as a result, ensues upon numerous adventures. Along with the story of Mickey and Lily Peaches is told the story of the Minturns, the wealthy and neglectful Mrs. Minturn, her not-so-well-to-do businessman husband, and their separation and return to happiness; all, of course, through the good offices of Mickey. A second love story, that of Leslie Winton and Douglas Bruce, is complicated by if not the chicanery then the unwisdom of her politician father who must make restitution of funds he has questionably diverted from their proper channels before his machinations are discovered. Mickey and Lily Peaches find a home in the country with Peter and Nancy Harding, who, while not childless, have room in their hearts for more. Through Mickey's influence the house, the home, and the family are rejuvenated. In fact, his maneuverings are so successful that a regular "Village Improvement Parade" takes place in the farm neighborhood rapidly becoming suburb where the Hardings live.

As a novel, this effort is without doubt Gene Stratton Porter's poorest. She is not at home in the city. Because of the book's setting, Multiopolis has to be Fort Wayne, Indiana, but her descriptions are of Philadelphia or New York, both of which she had visited by this time. Admittedly, the novelist has a perfect right to fictionalize her locale, but the patent unfamiliarity with big city life and ways mars the book. Her city streets lack the authenticity of her forest paths. And yet, when the story leaves the city, *Michael O'Halloran* contains some of the most descriptive of Porter's nature writing.

Through fern and brake head high, through sumac, willow, elder, buttonbush, gold-yellow and blood-red osiers, past northern holly, over spongy moss carpet of palest silvery green up-piled for ages, over red-veined pitcher plants spilling their fullness, among scraggy, odorous tamaracks, beneath which cranberries and rosemary were blooming; through ethereal pale mists of dawn, in their ears lark songs of morning from the fields, hermit thrushes in the swamp, bell birds tolling molten notes, in a minor strain a swelling chorus of sparrows, titmice, vireos, went two strong, healthy young people newly promised for better or worse.[12]

A Daughter of the Land published in 1918 completes the Indiana novels. Truly enough, *The White Flag* (1923) has a setting somewhere in the Central States, obviously Indiana, but in this book the setting is only incidental and plays no real part in the development of the story. *A Daughter of the Land* tells the struggle of Kate Bates to achieve a degree of equality with her brothers, each of whom upon attaining majority has received a gift of two hundred acres of land from his father (although the father has retained possession of the deeds). Kate has been denied this gift and even deprived of the brief period of schooling granted her older sisters. As the publishers' synopsis puts it, "She has helped earn so many two hundred acre farms for her brothers that her one ideal comes to be the possession of that number of acres for herself. The story follows her thru many years of struggle and disappointment to final achievement."[13]

But in reality there is little struggle in the book. If anything, rewards come too easily. Kate rebels against her father and is forced to leave his home, but her first attempt to borrow money for a summer's "Normal" schooling meets with success, as does her effort to secure a school for the winter term. Her second summer finds her befriended by an extremely wealthy woman from Chicago with an extremely wealthy and eligible son who, on first glance, is smitten by her and determined to marry her. She refuses him because he has not her love of the land and because (being a self-made man) he cannot write a decent letter. She marries a wastrel, George Holt, who hopes to get his hands on her father's fortune, not knowing, or refusing to believe, her father has disinherited her. Her father dies and Kate does receive a substantial inheritance. She invests it in a sawmill. First of all, George closes a sluice gate at the time of a spring freshet and destroys the dam; next, he blows up the boiler and himself along with it. Kate's inheritance gone, she is rescued by her mother who deeds to her a farm of considerably more that two hundred acres. Except for the interval with George, Kate really has a rather easy time of it.

A review of the book at the time of its publication stated: " 'A Daughter of the Land' is notable because it is simple and elemental, because it has sincerity and breadth, and because the story tells itself without resort to the artifices and trickery so often called to the aid of plots and scenes wanting in inherent spontaneity. The story is purely American in theme and inspiration."[14] One must take issue at least in part with this evaluation. The book employs practically every artifice and trick to make the plot move to its destined end. Robert Gray would have married Kate instead of her sister, Nancy Ellen, had he seen her first; accordingly, Nancy Ellen wrecks her car, killing herself, and leaving the way clear for Kate to marry Robert. John Jardine marries his mother's maid after Kate refuses him; years later, when they meet again, the healthy young wife conveniently dies, leaving Jardine free again. When George Holt has done his insufferable worst to Kate, he is blown up along with the boiler, thus making Kate a free (but impoverished) woman once more—at liberty to choose between John and Robert as each becomes available.

These are but a few examples, and the novel might well be called a pot-boiler. And yet Gene Stratton Porter in this book displays more of a gift for character building than in almost any of her other books. The waspish "Widder Holt" (a study in evil), the loquacious but kind-hearted Agatha, the vacillating Nancy Ellen, and the stern but honest Mother Bates are all sympathetically drawn. But it is the characterization of Kate herself which is a masterly study in contradiction. She is at once terse and self-centered yet inlooking and gentle. With an analytic and understanding intelligence, especially where others are concerned, she has the ability to make all the wrong choices as to what most concerns her. The result is a character blessed with a humanity not often encountered in Gene Stratton Porter's heroines.

There is a claim that Porter used events of her girlhood in this novel and that it is in a sense autobiographical.[15] The novel can be called autobiographical only if there is admitted to be such a thing as autobiography by antithesis. Father and Mother Bates are direct opposites in every way of Father and Mother Stratton, and Porter would be most unlikely to direct the acidulous portrayal she makes of the Bates against her own venerated parents. Kate Bates resembles Gene Stratton Porter only in her ability to struggle and to succeed. Finally, the farm itself is a dreary and forlorn place, not to be compared with the beloved Hopewell so faithfully depicted in *Laddie*. Porter in this novel exercised her power to imagine rather than to recall.

IV   *Nature in a New Land*

With the publication of *Her Father's Daughter* in 1921, Gene Stratton Porter's scene shifts to California. Linda Strong, the orphaned daughter of a sensitive and appreciative father, has inherited his qualities. Her half-sister, Eileen, has inherited all the selfish and ungracious traits of her mother. Linda achieves, much as did Elnora Comstock, the freedom and position she desires. There is a complication involving the plans for a perfect home that have been entered in a competition by Marian Thorne and a stealing of Marian's sweetheart by the voracious Eileen.

Linda is intent upon excelling in high school, but she is also intent on saving and preserving the flora of California, so rapidly falling before the developers. She is also interested in the preparation of food from native plants and under the name of Jane Meredith writes and sells recipes and nature notes. Here Porter predates Ewell Gibbons by some fifty years. Another facet of the book which makes it seem prophetic in view of later events is its strong anti-Japanese sentiment. In 1921 Gene Stratton Porter was ahead of her times.

A main point of interest for one studying the life of Gene Stratton Porter is that Linda Strong *is* Gene Stratton Porter. The Linda who gathers the plant life of California and makes it her own is the author to a much greater extent than was Elnora Comstock. And, as has been noted, the house in which Linda is so interested and the grounds surrounding it are the house and grounds Gene Stratton Porter planned for her permanent home. The book even contains a self-portrait:

As for Linda, Eileen never had considered her at all except as a convenience to serve her own purposes. Last night she had learned that Linda had a brain, that she had wit, that she could say things to which men of the world listened with interest. She began to watch Linda. She appraised with deepest envy the dark hair curling naturally on the temples. She wondered how hair that curled naturally could be so thick and heavy, and she thought what a crown of glory would adorn Linda's head when the day came to coil those long dark braids around it and fasten them with flashing pins. She drew some satisfaction from the sunburned face and lean figure before her, but it was not satisfaction of a soul-sustaining quality. There was beginning to be something disquieting about Linda. A roundness was creeping over her lean frame; a glow was beginning to colour her lips and cheek bones; a dewy look could be surprised in her dark eyes occasionally. She had the effect of a creature with something yeasty bottled inside it that was beginning to ferment and might effervesce at any minute.[16]

Anyone who has examined the girlhood portraits of Gene Stratton Porter as they are reproduced in the Meehan book or elsewhere can easily recognize the girl that Porter is depicting as Linda Strong, her father's daughter.

Linda Strong seems extremely precocious for a high-school girl. In addition to leading her classes, inspiring a boy in the school to excel over a Japanese student, and developing and publishing recipes for the use of native plants, she still has time to involve herself with a set of older people interested in architecture and romance. Gene Stratton Porter wrote her own boundless energy and multi-interests rather too vividly into the character of Linda Strong.

Her Father's Daughter is interesting for the new outlook on nature that Porter's recent acquaintance with California had engendered. Here was a profligacy never to be encountered in Indiana. While the Limberlost and its region were limited, this new land seemed limitless. There were ocean, mountain, desert, and canyon, and for each of them there was an abundance of bird and plant life to be studied and assimilated. Porter set out to conquer this vast array of natural history and to put it into her writing. Her Father's Daughter could almost serve as a guidebook for anyone wishing the experience of discovering the California of the 1920s—not of the cities, but of the countryside.

V   The Seamy Side of Life

Gene Stratton Porter maintained that The White Flag (1923) was her answer to those who claimed that she could write nothing but sugary romances and molasses fiction. Her daughter wrote:

Into this book Mother put more stark realism and more of the seamy side of life than any of her other books contain, and for this reason it proved less popular than many of the others. This only proved her own idea correct, which was that, after all, away down deep, the American people can be trusted to like the simple, beautiful things of humanity and nature. I believe she really wrote *The White Flag* just to see whether she was right or wrong, and to prove to some of the critics of her "sugary romances" that she was not ignorant of life's cesspools and could write about them if she chose.[17]

Although set in Indiana, *The White Flag* is not really one of the Indiana novels. It does not contribute to the picture Porter drew of her native state. In fact, the book is almost totally devoid of nature; there are only a few descriptions of the outdoors and what there are, are for the most part of the cultivated plants and flowers of the small town or of the farm.

While ostensibly the story of Mahala Spellman, *The White Flag* is really the story of the evil Martin Moreland and his equally evil son, Martin, Junior, and of the machinations to gain complete control of the little town of Ashwater. The novel traces the life histories of Mahala Spellman and Jason Peters and their associates through elementary and high school and into early adulthood. Mahala's refusal to marry Junior Moreland triggers a series of disasters for her, all brought about by the Morelands. Her father is financially ruined and dies of the realization; she and her mother lose everything and are forced to move into a house owned by a faithful servant; the Morelands accuse Mahala of theft because of the disappearance of a wallet (engineered by Junior); Mrs. Spellman dies of the shock; Mahala suffers typhoid, contracted in the jail; and finally removes to a farm salvaged from the wrecked Spellman fortune.

Parallel to this story is that of Jason Peters, the washerwoman's son. Derided by his schoolmates because of his poverty, sincerely hated by Junior, and befriended only by Mahala, he struggles onward and upward, becoming independent and the partner of Peter Potter in the grocery store which he transforms through his native talent into the town's leading establishment.

The demented Becky Sampson carries all the time the white flag of purity, imploring everyone to pass under it for salvation.

But the real story is that of Martin Moreland. Jason's supposed mother has been Martin's mistress. She has been forced to raise Jason but has never dared to let herself show any real affection from fear of Martin Moreland and from the certainty that some day he will be taken from her. Jason is actually—although this fact is not known until book's end—the legitimate son of Martin and Becky Sampson through "a real marriage but a fraudulent divorce." This, of course, makes Martin a bigamist and Junior a bastard, a fact which Porter leaves for her reader to deduce. The Moreland greed is overpowering and leads naturally to their downfall—Junior's suicide and Martin's dementia. It also leads to the clearing of Mahala's name.

Jason goes on loving Mahala and standing by her faithfully in all her trials. But, believing her guilty of the theft, he marries Ellen Ford, Mahala's neighbor, who bears his son. Then, Mahala's innocence having been proved, the two realize their love. From this welter, Porter's only recourse is to kill off Ellen, which she does melodramatically by striking her with lightning. The story ends with the insane Martin Moreland carrying Becky's white flag.

This book also marks Gene Stratton Porter's only extensive attempt at symbolism. The white flag is the symbol of purity, and the whole book is Porter's view of the need for and struggle for purification. What this purification is or how it is to be achieved—other than by wishing for it and making an outward show of acquiescence—Porter fails to expound clearly. The publisher's synopsis does little more to clear up the matter:

Martin Moreland, thru the power of money, holds the town of Ashwater in his grip. A daily evidence of his greed and secret sin is Rebecca, who in her demented state of mind bids all pass under her white flag and be purified. . . . In the final mad reaction of the townspeople against the Morelands all their sins are exposed and innocents cleared. Junior's suicide and his father's loss of reason alone save them from the mob. Ashwater calms down, Jason and Mahala are united, and Moreland thenceforth carries the white flag of Rebecca, true to her dying curse.[18]

The White Flag is different from other Porter novels, but not as different as she claimed it to be. She claimed to be writing realism but, if so, it is realism with a decidedly romantic flavor.

VI   *The Last Novels*

If Gene Stratton Porter deserted pleasantness for unpleasantness in *The White Flag*, she returned to it in *The Keeper of the Bees;* if *The White Flag* is almost devoid of nature, *The Keeper of the Bees* is redolent of it. No book, not even *The Harvester*, depends more on its natural setting than does *The Keeper of the Bees*. The book, published in 1925, concerns itself with a wounded war veteran, Jamie MacFarlane, who wanders away from an army hospital rather than face sure death in a tuberculosis camp. By sheerest coincidence he arrives at the home of the Beekeeper just as the latter is suffering a heart attack. Jamie assists him and takes over his place as the keeper of the bees. He is taught and ably assisted by the Little Scout, a sexless neighbor youngster. Another neighbor, Margaret Cameron, tends his wound, cooks his meals, and with the aid of good California air, sun and salt water, affects a cure.

Jamie envisions the Storm Girl who materializes but whose identity is concealed. She leads him into a marriage to give a fatherless baby-to-be a name. The baby is born but at the cost of the life of the mother; Jamie takes the baby and gives it over to the care of Margaret Cameron. There had been three children in Margaret Cameron's home, her daughter and two foster children, a girl and a boy. The daughter had loved her foster brother perhaps too well; when his death prevented their marriage, she found herself in the predicament from which Jamie, through the intervention of the Storm Girl, rescued her. The Storm Girl was, of course, the other child in the Cameron home. The baby turned out to be Margaret Cameron's grandson and entitled to a place in her affection and in her home.

A further complication arises with the death of the former beekeeper. He leaves his property equally to Jamie and the Little Scout. A young woman claiming to be the Beekeeper's daughter arrives and tries to take the inheritance; she is thoroughly routed by the Little Scout. This person, who has been the rather hoydenish leader of a group of equally boisterous boys, turns out to be a little girl, after all.

Perhaps no one of Porter's books excels this in nature description or in the use of nature for background. In addition to the picturing of the California coastal valley, there is the delineation of the bee garden itself. Porter had proved that she knew the swamps, forests, and fields of Indiana, and in *Her Father's Daughter* she showed that she was coming to have the same knowledge of the Los Angeles area. She had proved her erudition about birds, moths, and flowers; now she was proving an equal in-depth knowledge of bees. In the pages of this book one can detect the influence of her deep reading in Fabre and the major naturalists. But there is this difference; Porter puts her scientifically correct descriptions of the life and habits of the bees into the vernacular of the Little Scout. In an almost uninterrupted monologue of over sixteen pages, the Little Scout gives a complete and scientific life history of the bees.[19]

There is no record that *The Magic Garden* was either in the hands of the publishers or that it was completed before Porter's death. The account of Herbert R. Hill that "her daughter was beseeched to search her mother's desk for unpublished manuscripts" is likely, and Hill continues, "In 1925, *The Keeper of the Bees* and *Tales You Won't Believe* were published. In 1927 came *The Magic Garden* and a volume of essays, *Let Us Highly Resolve.*"[20] It is known that *The Keeper of the Bees* was completed and in the hands of the publishers by October 1924.[21] Meehan does say that her mother "wrote" *The Magic Garden* on Catalina Island in the fall of 1924, but there is a possibility that the tense should have been "was writing."

The book is one of the shortest of the novels. Only *The Song of the Cardinal* is shorter, and *At the Foot of the Rainbow* equals it in length. All the other novels are at least four hundred pages, and *Laddie* reaches six hundred. This shortness might well indicate the *The Magic Garden* was unfinished at Porter's death and was arranged and completed by Meehan or someone else. But there is a claim that such is not the case. A letter from Mrs. Hathaway states that *The Magic Garden* had been completed but not sold before Porter's death because she did not want anything else too soon after *The Keeper of the Bees*. The first installment of this novel appeared in *McCall's* in February 1925 and the book publication was scheduled for August of the same year. Finished or unfinished, the novel is almost puerile in plot and characterization. Porter had grown—at least in craftsman-ship—and this book lacks the polish she undoubtedly would have given it. It seems almost certain that there would have been more work done on the manuscript if it were not for the accident that took her life.

When the story begins, the heroine, Amaryllis, is a child of five in a wealthy but broken home. Unloved, cared for by indifferent servants, and tantrumish, she runs away and finds happiness for a while with John Guido, a lonely boy only a few years her senior and a budding violinist, in the magic garden surrounding his home. She is recovered by her father who, cognizant of his neglect, determines to become a real parent. The remainder of the book traces the growing up of Amaryllis and her development into young womanhood. Never forgetting John Guido she keeps track of him and watches his progress toward successful professional musicianship. Amaryllis prepares for his homecoming to the magic garden only to learn of his supposed death in a yachting accident. With typical Porter convenience, the rumor is proved to be false—he missed the boat—and in the magic garden, Amaryllis learns that John Guido has never forgotten her.

This last novel of Gene Stratton Porter's is set neither in Indiana nor in California but apparently on Long Island. But there is little in the book to characterize it as belonging particularly to anywhere. The island is a place purely of her imagination although she had visited it when she spent an afternoon with Theodore Roosevelt.[22] She is no more at home in cities than she was in *Michael O'Halloran,* and her descriptions of the estates dotting the island are only vaguely drawn and lack conviction. She makes great use of both the flower and of Lully's air, "Amaryllis," as sentimental bonds between the lovers. But then, Lully's (if it was his) tune has had a consistent appeal for over three hundred years, and John Guido's use of it in a concert was not so different from Galli Curci's fondness for "Home, Sweet Home" and "The Last Rose of Summer." The popular taste of the 1920s still favored Ethelbert Nevin's "Narcissus" and "The Rosary" or Leybach's "Fifth Nocturne" over Mahler and Strauss (Richard, not Johann).

These, then, are the novels of Gene Stratton Porter. Inconsequential as they may be to the mainstream of American literature, and overly sentimental and romantic as they are, they are still deserving of a more careful consideration and evaluation than they have received.

CHAPTER 4

The Books of the Outdoors

I   *The Books of the Birds*

THE nature writing of Gene Stratton Porter is not nearly so extensive as an examination of her published titles would lead one to assume. The books—those dealing primarily with birds—were for the most part reissues and revisions of her first series of bird essays, *What I Have Done with Birds,* which appeared in the *Ladies' Home Journal* in five issues from April to August of 1906, and which were published in book form under the same title by Bobbs-Merrill in 1907. But five essays were not enough for a respectable-sized book, and to them were added others, some of which had appeared in *Outing* and *Metropolitan,* and some of which most likely were written specifically for this volume.

For some reason, Gene Stratton Porter was dissatisfied with *What I Have Done with Birds* (or perhaps she wanted to bring this collection under the aegis of her new publishers, Doubleday, Page & Company), and in 1917 a revised and enlarged edition was published entitled *Friends in Feathers.* Of the twenty-five essays in this volume, nineteen were—with only slight revision—taken from *What I Have Done with Birds;* there were six new studies.

Then, in 1919, came *Homing with the Birds.* In this book, no essays—with the exception of "A Gift of the Birds" from the *Youth's Companion*—were reprinted, but the whole volume draws heavily on material which had previously been used. There is, of course, much new material, or material so rewoven as to appear new, and there is much more of Gene Stratton Porter—of the woman rather than the naturalist—and her family than was in the earlier volumes.

In 1923 came a third offering of the "bird" studies of Gene Stratton Porter. This was called simply *Wings* and was her own selection and editing of what she considered best from *What I Have Done with Birds, Friends in Feathers,* and *Homing with the Birds.* There is nothing in this book which had not appeared elsewhere.

Tales You Won't Believe, which was published in 1925, also contains bird studies and bird stories. Of the fifteen sketches in the book, eight are about birds, while the remaining seven cover a variety of subjects ranging from moths and flowers to personal reminiscence. Much of the material recounts incidents from previous publications although in slightly different guise, but much is new, at least to book form.

There were other nature books by Gene Stratton Porter in which this pattern of repetition was not so apparent. There was even another book about birds, *Birds of the Bible,* and *Music of the Wild,* a book which contains much reference to birds, especially to bird song. *Moths of the Limberlost* completes the list of nature books and is, as its name implies, about the author's experience with moths and has little or nothing to do with birds.

"What I Have Done with Birds" was the title given to the series of bird studies that Gene Stratton Porter agreed to do for Edward W. Bok, the famous editor of the *Ladies' Home Journal.* When these essays were issued along with some others in book form the title was retained. The subtitle, "Character studies of native American birds which through friendly advances I induced to pose for me, or succeeded in photographing by good fortune, with the story of my experiences in obtaining the pictures," fully explains what the book is about.

The book, quite naturally, is highly personal and as informative of the author as it is of her subjects. With what patience and what painstaking care she worked to secure these bird pictures. Gene Stratton Porter had made of herself a masterful photographer; the book is lavishly illustrated with seventeen full-page colored plates and with numerous black and white pictures.

It would not be too difficult to enumerate and to catalog the nature experiences of Gene Stratton Porter, for it seems certain that they were all used and in many cases used repeatedly. Perhaps the experience which made the greatest impression on her was the discovery of the black vulture's nest and the series of photographs she made of the developing chick. This story is one of the chapters in *What I Have Done with Birds* which appeared in the *Ladies' Home Journal,* but it had also appeared in *Outing* in December 1901 and in *Metropolitan* in April 1902. The sketch and the photographs, used and reused, are repeated in *Friends in Feathers*, in *Homing with the Birds*, in *Wings*, and in *Music of the Wild*; furthermore, it is the motivation for the appearance of the Bird Woman and the Swamp Angel in *Freckles*. One wonders if the readers of Gene Stratton Porter were so faithful that they would accept so much repetition or if each new book reached a different audience, one unfamiliar with the previous books.

The case of the vulture is but one instance that could be cited. The stories of the orioles' nest with a window and the photographing of the belted kingfisher come to mind. But, in spite of her working and reworking her territory, there remains a considerable bulk of nature writing.

The sketches which comprise *What I Have Done with Birds* are all of a pattern. A particular bird is selected for each, and the author tells of her experiences in securing the set of photographs she was after. Her intention was to photograph as much of the life cycle of the birds as she possibly could. With the cameras and equipment which were available to her at that time, she was pretty much limited to those activities which were localized. She could not follow the flight of birds or capture their feeding or migration. Her studies had to be centered around one particular spot—the nest. She could only record the building of the nest (often including at least a part of the courtship), the eggs in the nest, the brooding, and the development of the fledglings until they were able to leave the nest and fend for themselves.

Her writing method was narrative, anecdotal, and highly personal. The stories are first person, and the manner while reportorial is relaxed, even chatty. Much criticism was leveled against Gene Stratton Porter that she was too assured of herself, too proud of her own achievements.[1] And yet she had every right to be proud. No other woman—no other naturalist, for that matter—had accomplished what she had with the photographing of the birds. There were others who had done and were doing more valuable scientific work, but they had not the fine gift of presenting their work and their observations in a combination of words and pictures which would appeal to a great many people. Those others could be grateful to her; her readers who found pleasure in the popular and pleasant accounts of nature in her writing might well be induced to read *them*.

Friends in Feathers, as has been stated, was an enlarged and

revised edition of *What I Have Done with Birds.* In the nineteen
sketches reprinted from the earlier volume, the revision is,
indeed, slight; the title article is changed to agree with the new
book, but the content is little altered. Six more birds are dealt
with, but in the same conversational, leisurely manner of the
original nineteen.

Homing with the Birds (1919) is a much more ambitious effort
than either *Friends in Feathers* or its predecessor, and is without
doubt the best of the Porter nature books. It was of this book that
Christopher Morley wrote his well-known letter of appreciation
to Mr. F. N. Doubleday:

> To-night I came across a copy of *Homing with the Birds* lying on the
> desk of Dr. Douglas, our literary editor. I picked it up and have been
> spending fascinating hours with it when I ought to have been doing
> some urgent work.
>
> It is a book to be proud of, and I can hardly tell you how deep and
> complex a pleasure it has given me—something of the breathless
> satisfaction one feels on those rare occasions when one knows one's self
> following along some path toward the magic of truth. Mrs. Porter's
> beautiful stories of her bird friends, some of them pathetic, some of
> them humorous, are a kind of education in the art of wondering at the
> fulness of life. They refresh the sense of amazement. What could be
> more touching than the story of the robin that stayed in her nest during
> ninety hours of rain? Or more entertaining than the anecdote of the
> wastrel waxwing so gloriously drunk on pokeberry wine?
>
> I cannot see that Mrs. Porters great work with birds is any inferior to
> the studies of the famous Fabre with insects. I hope the book will have
> the greatest possible success. A book of that sort does one as much good
> as (or perhaps more than) going to church. If the essence of religion is
> an attitude of reverence toward mysteries too great for us to
> understand, then this book has in it the gist of many creeds.
>
> Please pardon this outburst! It is a spontaneous utterance of
> admiration for Mrs. Porter's unique gift of fellowship with the birds,
> which seems to have been born in her warm and courageous heart.[2]

Mrs. Porter liked to infer that the letter was in commendation of
all her work, but it resulted from Morley's having picked up the
volume, read it, and written of his experienc to Mr. Doubleday.

All of *Homing with the Birds* is of the life of Gene Stratton
Porter, but the opening chapters are purely autobiographical.
The first chapters tell of her early childhood and of how her
parents instilled in her the love of nature in all its aspects,

especially the birds and flowers. Not only did she learn to love
nature, but the principles of conservation were taught to her by
her father:

As I recall, there were small flocks of birds for every *one* that is seen at
the present time. We were taught to love the song birds for their
beauty, their music, and the likeness of their life processes to ours. We
were told that we must not harm a bird's nest because it would break
the little mother bird's heart; but no one every particularly impressed
it upon us to protect them because the berry and fruit crops would fail
if we did not. My father was the only person I ever heard mention this
subject in my childhood. The birds' work as insect exterminators was
not generally realized or taught at that time, while the spraying of fruit
trees was unknown.[3]

Porter speaks of the extreme plentitude of wild life in her
childhood, of the passenger pigeons soon to become extinct.
Quail were so numerous that eggs were taken for the table and
the birds were trapped. In cold weather there was always an
ample supply of wild turkey, prairie chicken, squirrel, and rabbit
hanging frozen in the woodshed.

The autobiographical introductory chapters of *Homing with
the Birds* are followed by others dealing with the lure of field
work, her unusual experiences in the field, the securing of rare
pictures, and her interpretations of bird life—their language,
songs, courtship, nest building, and like concerns. It would be
unfair to qualify this part of the book as disjointed or rambling. It
was the author's intention to present in no chronological order a
series of anecdotes dealing with her experiences with birds and
all related to her central thesis; that they are marvellous and
valuable creatures worthy of a fairer consideration by man.

The style is conversational; Mrs. Porter is simply relating what
happened in straightforward exposition as she would to any
interested listener. And in so doing, she was able to avoid that
element for which she was most criticized—her overburgeoning
sentimentality. She makes it obvious that she is telling of that in
which she is intensely interested, and so contagious is her
enthusiasm that the reader is equally engrossed. The accounts
are for the most part devoid of that anthropopathy which mars
much of her work. She is so intent on the current happening, on
her real involvement in the situation, that she does not humanize
her subjects as she did on other occasions when she attempted to

make something—either fiction or nature article or poem—out of these experiences gathered in the actual environment of nature.

It seems that Gene Stratton Porter had to keep reminding herself that birds do not actually possess the human attributes that she finds it so easy to endow them with. As is quite natural, she finds it easier to detect this fault in the nature writing of others than in her own. She knew quite well that ". . .poetic interpretations and romancing make beautiful reading but bad natural history."[4] When she succumbed to this temptation, as she did in many places in "What the Birds Say and Sing," her writing was at its worst, but it must be remembered that it might also be at its most popular with many of her readers. When she resisted the temptation, her writing was at its best. Her powers of observation were so keen and her descriptions so accurate that she could vie with the scientists for veracity while at the same time remaining readable. For example, consider her description of the wood duck:

Linnaeus called this duck "the bride," but he should have explained that the male wore the nuptial dress and that the dress was that of the most colourful orientals; for this loveliest of our ducks is as gorgeous in dress as "Solomon in all his glory." My bird's beak, with its very dark, hooked, pointed tip, had a triangle of blood red on each side at the base; from that a wide irregular mark of pale yellow ran down its sides. The top of his head was exquisite. It was pure green of several shades in places, bronze-maroon in others, bronzy green between. White lines ran from the red at the base of the beak above the eye on each side to the tip of the long crest, which hung far down the back of the neck. Secondary lines of white started back of the eyes and ended with the crest. The eyes were large, having wide circles of red around the iris. The cheeks and sides of the head were dark bronze. The throat was snow white, this colour rounding the cheek and running up to the eye in a narrow strip, again circling the side of the head and coming to a point at the crest. The white came far down the throat, and stopped in an even line where the breast changed to a lovely shade of maroon, lighter than that of the head, yet having the same bronzy tints. This broad band covered the back of the neck below the shoulders, shading lighter over the crop, where it was flecked with almost invisible feathers of white at the top, the line widening and the feathers growing larger where they met the white underparts. At the wing butts, a narrow band of white faced the maroon, then one twice as wide of black; then came delicate pale yellow feathers finely traced with black, and broader

bands of black and white. The back was green overlaid with maroon
and hints of yellow, with a white band across the top of the tail base,
the tail very long for a duck, green above, maroon at the sides. The feet
were invisible in the water.[5]

Compare this passage with the description of the same bird by
one of the most prominent ornithologists of the time:

. . . Head, including crest, irridescent green and purple; a narrow
white line from bill over eye to rear of crest; another commencing
behind eye and running to nape; a broad white patch on throat forking
behind, one streak curving upward behind eye, the other curving on
side of neck; above, lustrous violet and bronzy green; shoulders and
long inner secondaries, velvet-black glossed with purple and green; a
greenish blue speculum bounded by white tips of secondaries behind;
primaries, white-edged and frosted on webs near end; upper tail-
coverts and tail deep dusky black; *sides and front of lower neck and
breast, rich purplish-chestnut evenly marked with small V-shaped
white spots;* a large black crescent in front of wing preceded by a white
one; sides yellowish-gray waved with fine black bars; rest of *under
parts white;* lengthened flank feathers falling in a tuft of rich purplish-
red below wing; bill, white in center, black on ridge, tip, and below,
with a square patch of lake-red; feet, yellowish-orange; iris and lids,
crimson.[6]

Homing with the Birds is filled with pleas for the protection of
birds; of the wood duck, of the passenger pigeon, which was
believed to be not quite extinct, of the wild turkey, and of the
owls and other birds of prey. And her concern extended beyond
the birds. "If men do not take active conservation measures soon,
I shall be forced to enter politics to plead for the conservation of
the forests, wildflowers, the birds and over and above everything
else, the precious water on which our comfort, fertility and life
itself depend."[7]

The idea of conservation is implicit in all of the nature writing
of Gene Stratton Porter, but it becomes very explicit in *Homing
with the Birds.* The final chapter, "Shall We Pay Our Debt," is an
eloquent plea for the preservation of bird life, not for aesthetic
or sentimental reasons but out of economic necessity. She
foresaw Rachel Carson's "silent spring" by half a century,
although her world without birds resulted directly from man's
greed and lack of understanding rather than indirectly from his
poisoning with insecticides. She presented a catalog of the birds

and of the particular benefits of each species, enumerating the weeds and insects they destroy. She launched a tirade against the English sparrow and the cowbird because of their destruction of other birds' nests and young and urged the complete extermination of them—an event which has not taken place. Another evidence of her modernity is her championship of the birds of prey—the eagles, hawks, and owls—and of the vultures, and her stressing of the necessity for the protection and preservation of these species because of their importance in the great scheme of nature. One interesting suggestion she made which would not popularize her with law-enforcement officers of today was that "if you have a small waste place, where a handful of hemp seed can be sowed in spring and seed raised to add to suet and meat bones for the birds in winter, that will be a great help, since the seed is very rich in oil and a warming food for birds."[8] Now, the hemp she was referring to was none other than marijuana; no wonder her birds were happy birds.

Birds of the Bible (1909) was one of Gene Stratton Porter's most ambitious projects, and the book itself one of the most lavish produced by her publishers. It was also one of the least successful of her books and is perhaps the most unreadable of all her work from the modern reader's standpoint. The author attempted to isolate references to birds in the Bible, to identify them, and to relate them to their present-day counterparts. Her father was a student of the Bible, and she knew it well, but she was by no means a scholar of the Bible. No more was she endowed with a firsthand knowledge of biblical lands. In a letter (to whom not known) concerning *Birds of the Bible* she says that her investigation ". . .led to the search for the dawn of bird history, and the very first pictures preserved ever made of birds. It was a merry chase, and it led me *around the world* [italics supplied] through books and galleries and museums."[9] In spite of this claim, there is no evidence of Gene Stratton Porter ever having visited the Holy Land. Now, "around the world" is most certainly hyperbolic, but the "books and galleries and museums" must have been real. And while much of this kind of research could have been done in Indianapolis or Chicago, her quest would have most logically led her to New York City and to the Library of Congress, the Smithsonian, and other collections in Washington.

In *Tales You Won't Believe,* published in 1925 but referring to the time she was living in Geneva and at about the same time she was writing *Birds of the Bible*, Porter says in an attempt to authenticate her reporting of English skylarks in Indiana, ". . .But I have never been abroad."[10] It has been established that Mrs. Porter could write well only from that which she knew. She knew Indiana; she did not know Palestine. The birds of the Bible became the birds of the Limberlost bearing similar names, and birds alien to America—the peacock, the hoopoe, the stork, the ostrich, and the raven—appear on her pages as they must have appeared in the museums from which she secured her illustrations: dead, dusty, and stuffed. It is also apparent from the book that Mrs. Porter's interpretation of the biblical scene was inspired by her native land; it was not until years later that she came to realize that the Holy Land was probably somewhat more like Southern California than like Indiana.[11]

It is puzzling to one who wants to know the life of Gene Stratton Porter to find that there is so little reference to any of the trips she must have taken. Allusions are made, as those just discussed in connection with *Birds of the Bible*, but there is little direct statement and an almost total absence of dates. There are references to her having gone to the Chicago World's Fair in 1893 and to her having visited Buffalo and in various locations in Pennsylvania when her daughter had married G. Blaine Monroe (or Munroe) and was living there. A business trip to Cincinnati is referred to, and her letters speak of field work in Michigan and Illinois as well as in Indiana. She did make a trip to Nebraska for *Country Life* to write an article about a model ranch, and this article was published in January 1907.

As far as research for *Birds of the Bible* is concerned, there is no real evidence of her having visited New York prior to the time this book was being written. She speaks of her friendship for Neltje Blanchan (pen name of the wife of the head of her publishing house, Mr. F. N. Doubleday, and a nature writer herself) and writes in the Introduction to *Homing with the Birds* that in the fall of 1916 she visited in the home of F. N. Doubleday. Meehan reports that her mother spent the summer of 1919 "visiting in the East, mostly with Dr. Emerson and his wife in Clifton Springs, New York.[12] The incident of the engaging newsboy that inspired *Michael O'Halloran* took place according to Porter on a New York street.[13] But Meehan places the event in Philadelphia in an account of an impossible occurrence. *"In the fall of 1915* [italics supplied] we moved to Philadelphia, and Father and Mother spent Thanksgiving of that year with us. . . .One afternoon, as we were hurrying home from a shopping trip, a little newsboy paused beside us and asked us to buy a paper. . . . After she went home Mother wrote a book, *Michael O'Halloran,* based on this incident. *It was published in August, 1915* [italics supplied] and is the story of a plucky little newsboy."[14] In all fairness to Meehan, she corrects herself a page or two later by placing the visit more believably in 1914.

But all these events were subsequent to the writing of *Birds of the Bible.*

Other sources give a few more clues to the travels of Gene Stratton Porter. In *Tales You Won't Believe* she states, "I am very familiar with Walden Pond as Thoreau saw it." This statement is somewhat ambiguous; she may have seen it with her own eyes or through Thoreau's eyes by reading *Walden.* An account in a local newspaper tells of her being invited to England to work with H. A. Saintsbury on a dramatization of *Freckles* for Dorothea Desmond. While the article assumes that she would make the trip, there is no evidence that she did.[15] The statement in *Tales You Won't Believe* that she had never been abroad must be remembered, and her grandniece, Mrs. Hathaway, states definitely that Gene Stratton Porter "never traveled abroad or even extensively in the U.S."

But does "abroad" include Mexico? There is one bit of evidence of travel—although questionable—in Limberlost Cabin North. This is the living-room fireplace "where a number of minature carved stone Aztec heads, collected by Mr. Porter in Mexico, are set amidst the stone work."[16] Another source states that these stones were collected by *the Porters* in Mexico.[17] But there is no further proof of Mr. Porter's visit nor any suggestion as to whether or not the excursion occurred before or after his marriage nor any mention of Gene Stratton Porter having been with him; there are today Mexican and Indian relics at Limberlost North.

Lorene (Miller) Wallace, Gene Stratton Porter's secretary for many years (1908-15), tells of visits from Mr. and Mrs. F. N. Doubleday, from Edward W. Bok, and from Honore Wiltsie Morrow, managing editor of the *Delineator* and author of Lincoln historical novels, and suggests—but only suggests—that these were return visits.[18]

Although the evidence itself is fragmentary, indisputably the books of Gene Stratton Porter are not the books of a well-traveled author, nor does travel play much of a part in any of the novels. But the nature books and the nature portions of the novels tell a different story. Both present an extremely detailed and intimate depiction of the country as contrasted with the rather sketchy and limited portrayal of the city. The reader sees, hears, and experiences Gene Stratton Porter's countryside while city streets and city life are only vaguely pictured. The books are provincial rather than cosmopolitan. And so it is with *Birds of the Bible;* the evidence does not point to wide travel experience in the life of the author.

At any rate, much to Mrs. Porter's disappointment, *Birds of the Bible* failed to sell. With the exception of *After the Flood,* which was a commissioned work, and *What I Have Done with Birds,* which was reissued under a new title, *Birds of the Bible* is the only book by Gene Stratton Porter never published by Doubleday. The novels, *Freckles* and *A Girl of the Limberlost,* had been published by this company in 1904 and 1909 respectively, and *The Song of the Cardinal* was to see its first appearance under the Doubleday logo in 1910. But *Birds of the Bible* was brought out by the Cincinnati firm of Jennings and Graham (Eaton & Mains, New York) in 1909. The book, with its heavy, enameled paper, its expensive pictorial, wood-grained cover, its slip cover, and its eighty-one photographic illustrations must have been almost prohibitively expensive to produce. One can only suppose that Gene Stratton Porter herself invested heavily in this book, for the Cincinnati firm did not have the sales of the novels to offset the cost. The much touted arrangement with her publishers to alternate novels with nature books must have come after 1909. Starting with *Moths of the Limberlost* in 1912, all subsequent publication of Porter's work was from Doubleday. Jennings and Graham owned the copyright to *Music of the Wild* and published it in only a slightly less expensive format than *Birds of the Bible* in 1910. But almost identical volumes were issued by Doubleday in 1910 and 1911, and there seems to have been simultaneous publication in England and in Canada.[19]

There is no need for a discussion of *Wings* (1923), since it was a reprinting of selections from other books. It is of interest in that it presents what Porter considered her best writing about her lifelong association with the birds. They had served her well, and she had returned the service by winning for them millions of friends among those in whom she had awakened or reawakened an interest in nature.

II   *The Book of the Moths*

Moths of the Limberlost was considered by Gene Stratton Porter to be her crowning achievement in writing of nature. And so it was—for her time. But it is in the illustration of the book rather than in its content that the volume is outstanding. Plagued by the limitation of black and white photography, Mrs. Porter set out to overcome the lack of color—so necessary for the depiction of moths—by supplying color. She chose watercolor as her medium.

Porter became interested in moths as an outgrowth of her work with birds. The many hours she spent patiently waiting for the right moment to click her shutter or squeeze her bulb were not wasted hours. She engaged herself with the numerous other evidences of natural history proliferating about her. She became fascinated with the great velvety-winged creatures of the June night in the Limberlost.

Mrs. Porter never seemed to take the same interest in butterflies that she did in moths. Perhaps, because they were creatures of the daytime, they had to face the competition from her beloved birds. Perhaps they were less spectacular than their big night-flying cousins. But it is more likely that it was because the life cycle of butterflies is less easy to study than that of moths. The cocoons of the latter, prominently displayed on twigs or branches, are things of beauty and interest in themselves. To watch the emergence of the moth from the cocoon, and to watch the almost incredibly rapid growth of the maturing wings is entrancing. It is also a simpler process to trace the life history of the moth than of the butterfly. The mating process can be observed, the eggs collected and hatched, the caterpillars nurtured, and the whole miracle of metamorphosis recorded with the camera.

Not all moths emerge from cocoons. There are many which overwinter in pupae cases in the ground as do most butterflies, but the cases are much larger and the "raising" of the moths much easier. And then there is the fascination of watching the mature caterpillar undergo the transformation from larva to pupa, the spinning of the cocoon, or the hardening of the case.

Anyone at all familiar with the work of Gene Stratton Porter will know that *ease* was never a determining factor in anything she set out to accomplish. *Moths of the Limberlost* was by no means an easy book to produce. Once an interest had been aroused in Mrs. Porter, she studied her subject thoroughly. Poring through book after book about Lepidoptera, she was struck by the inadequacy of the illustrations. "Scientists from the beginning have had no hesitation in using dead and pinned moth specimens for book illustrations, despite the fact that the colours are faded, the wings in unnatural positions, and the body shrivelled. I would quite as soon accept the mummy of any particular member of the Rameses family as a fair representative of the living man as accept a mounted moth for a living one. All the illustrations in my moth book are made from living moths and caterpillars in perfectly natural positions in which they placed themselves."[20]

To secure these illustrations was a herculean task. Getting the pictures, although painstaking and time-consuming, was no particular problem, but the reproduction of the color was a more difficult chore. Since the samples returned for the color presses were unsatisfactory, she set about producing her own colored drawings. The publishers could reproduce faithfully from a colored picture; they could not achieve satisfactory results from descriptions or samples.

Gene Stratton Porter's early training and self-instruction in painting stood her in good stead. She was by no means a master of watercolor but she made herself one. She had made the colored illustrations for *The Song of the Cardinal* and had acquired a great deal of skill in this endeavor. But the subtlety of the coloration of moths demanded special technique and meticulous, time-consuming attention to detail. But she was a master in patience and perserverance. She secured the finest watercolors and brushes available and experimented with the mixing of color until she could reproduce with complete accuracy any nuance of shade or hue. She experimented with print papers until she found a platinum paper which would give a distinct but unobtrusive image and a surface suitable for watercolor. Meehan tells that she brought down from the attic the easel which her father had had made for when she first dabbled in oil painting. The watercolorist usually works on a flat surface, not at an easel, but nowhere is there given a detailed description as to how Porter painted her moths. Her work was not suggestive but was actual mimicry of nature. The velvety coverings of the wings and bodies of moths consist of minute overlapping scales (which she often calls feathers), and she painted her specimens almost scale by scale. She tells of "dawdling hours over painting a moth wing with a brush trimmed to three hairs!"[21]

If the illustration of *Moths of the Limberlost* is compared with that of other nature books of the period, its magnificence is clearly recognizable. These pictures are alive and vibrant. Even today, the book suffers little in comparison with the miracles achieved by modern photography and printing.

The text of *Moths of the Limberlost* is typical of Gene Stratton Porter. With the same careful observation, the same keen enthusiasm in her interest, and the same gift for recounting her experiences, she deals with the moths as she had dealt with birds and flowers. The book is not and was never intended to be a scientific treatise. It is limited in its scope, being confined by the definition of the title to a rather restricted area of Northeastern Indiana and the moths to be found there. It is intended for the nature lover rather than the scientific naturalist. In telling of her own adventures with moths, Porter is telling her readers how by like activities they may experience the same sorts of things for themselves. A book review of the time states that "the nature lover rather than the naturalist in the strictest sense of the word has been kept in mind thruout the preparation of the work, whose aim is to teach the former how to identify the moths he finds, to explain whether they are creatures of light or darkness, whether they accomplish their mission without nourishment, where to find them, what are their habits, where to look for their winter quarters, and to give them a name that can be readily remembered."[22]

A comparison between *Moths of the Limberlost* and *A Girl of the Limberlost* is inevitable. Although *A Girl of the Limberlost* was published in 1909 and *Moths of the Limberlost* not until 1912, the field work for both books must have been done before the publication of the former. Perhaps the painstaking work of producing the watercolor illustrations for *Moths of the Limberlost* delayed the publication of this book. Other than the experience of Mrs. Porter in having become the perfect moth bait by having been sprayed with a liquid from the abdomen of a female Cecropia, which is repeated when Kate Comstock goes into the swamp at night to try to recover the moth she had destroyed, there is little direct repetition, but there are many experiences which are common to both books. There is also a degree of correspondence with *Tales You Won't Believe*. The "moth bait" incident is retold, and the story of the Limberlost's rarest moth is repeated.[23]

It is not known whether Gene Stratton Porter herself dealt in supplying specimens for collectors as did Elnora Comstock. Elnora sold mainly to the Bird Woman, who was conducting a thriving enterprise world-wide. Now, the Bird Woman is always Gene Stratton Porter, and in an article in *Country Life* she appends a list of prices of cocoons and pupae cases and the names and addresses of collectors and other parties wanting to buy or exchange specimens.[24] If she was not actually engaged in the business, she was at least familiar with the market.

Even today, *Moths of the Limberlost* is an easily readable and reliable introduction to moths and moth collecting. In spite of being limited to a small section of Indiana, the moths it discusses are to be found over a wide area of North America. It is easy to identify specimens by comparing them with Porter's carefully colored illustrations. But perhaps the greatest contribution of the book was that it taught thousands of people to understand and appreciate a facet of nature which was practically unknown to them. For many children (and grown-ups as well) it could dispel the fear of worms and caterpillars and dispel the fears of many for darkness and night.

III   *The Books of Nature*

Music of the Wild is, with the possible exception of *Homing with the Birds*, one of Gene Stratton Porter's most delightful books. One of the things that makes it so is the lavish use of her own photography, not only as illustration, but as a key to the text. There are 119 full-page plates. This number is not particularly in excess of other books, but the difference lies in the fact that these pictures display Gene Stratton Porter's talents as a photographer of subjects other than birds. Less than a quarter of these pictures are of birds. With the same meticulous care and artistic composition which mark her bird studies, she presents insects. flowers, trees, and—above all—landscapes.

These landscapes tell one better than words the settings for the nature books and nature novels of Gene Stratton Porter, and especially they reconstruct the past. The rural Indiana of the early years of the century comes alive. Here are dirt roads unfenced or graced by rail fences but with never a sign of wire, either in fencing or in telephone, telegraph, or power lines. Here are streams and rivers unpolluted by man. Here are sketches of woodland with trees such as are seldom seen today. And here is the swampland with its slow meandering creeks and quiet pools. There are pictures of the buildings erected by man in a time long past even in Gene Stratton Porter's day. For within this lonely and withdrawn region, people still lived much as they had in the days of the settlement. In this book are recorded pictorially these nostalgic reminders of time long past and of a time which can never be recaptured except in records such as this.

The entire book is as redolent of color as it is of sound. The regret arises that Mrs. Porter did not live in the time of modern color photography so that she might have portrayed the sweeps of color that she describes so vividly. But the regret is shortlived. Being deprived of the aid of color, the artist is forced to concentrate on composition and values to achieve a delicate balance between light and shade, to employ such skill that the essence of the subject is inescapable. This feat Mrs. Porter accomplishes time and time again.

Music of the Wild is written in three sections. The first is devoted to the forest, the second to the fields, and the third to the marsh or swamp. Music—or the sound of nature—is a unifying theme which runs throughout the book and holds together a collection of vignettes on otherwise seemingly unrelated subjects, although the actual progression through forest, field, and marsh provides another thread of unification. In spite of this framework it almost seems as if the author is so full of her subject, and her love for nature and the outdoors so abounding, that she must set down, rather chaotically, all the thoughts that occur to her. It is a book that need not be read through from cover to cover; it is, rather, a book to pick up and turn to any page and read, being sure that some interesting bit of nature lore will be forthcoming. And the pictures are not just stuck in to "illustrate" the book; they are keyed to the text by use of marginal captions, often the same as the title of the photograph, so that the reader is led immediately to the description of that portion of forest, field, or marsh being illustrated.

"The Chorus of the Forest" describes the great wood and its inhabitants, not in its primeval state, for the encroachments of man had begun before Gene Stratton Porter's time, but while huge trees still remained. The cutting which had been done had been to supply the needs of farms and villages in the immediate vicinity, not to satisfy the demands of the furniture factories in Grand Rapids.

Of the forest Porter says, "Cutting your path before you means clearing it of living things as well as removing the thicket of undergrowth. A hundred little creatures are fleeing at your every step, and wherever you set your foot you kill without your knowledge; for earth, leaves, and mosses are teeming with life. You need only press your ear to the ground and lie still to learn that a volume of sound is rising to heaven from the creeping, crawling, voiceless creatures of earth, the minor tone of all its music."[25]

It is in this spirit that Gene Stratton Porter takes her reader into the forest. She is attentive and observing. She is concerned, of course, with the trees—with the forest itself—but she is even more concerned with the undergrowth and the flowers and other vegetation of the forest floor. She presents almost a catalog of the birds, the small animals, the insects, and the wildflowers to be found in the forest. The overriding purpose, the unifying theme of the book, is to present the sounds of nature and to show that the individual voices combine to make up a veritable euphony of music.

When, in "The Songs of the Fields," she moves from the forest to the farmland, Gene Stratton Porter is again dealing with what for modern readers is a distant past. These are not the fields of modern agriculture. There are no vast acreages, no miles of wire fencing, no great tractors and combines; there are instead the small plots capable of being worked with horses, there are the great staples—corn and oats, and there are the meadows and pastures and woodlots. Untamed nature is not remote from these fields; they are surrounded by the raw outdoors, and nature is always encroaching on cultivation. Such a rural setting is ideal for the devotee of nature study and natural history, but it is also for the most part only a remembrance of America's more romantic past.

The contrast between the forest and the fields is, of course, the contrast between light and dark, between sunshine and shadow. The plants and animals (and birds and insects are animals) which thrive in openness and light are to be found here.

We are not dealing with model farms, and so in the beginning the upturned earth of my oat field is beautiful, because at the heels of the plowman follow larks, blackbirds, bluebirds, and robins picking grubs; and the warm spring air is vibrant with their notes. The field is enclosed with a straggling old snake-fence overgrown with carrion vine and moonseed; the corners filled with alder, wild rose, milkweed, saffron, and wild mustard, and interlaced with dodder in myriads of fine gold threads. There are big forest trees all around it, making a hedge reaching heavenward. Every insect and bird of the field homes there, and the river singing along one side adds not only its voice, but the notes of kingfisher, killdeer, sheilpoke, and sandpiper.[26]

That Gene Stratton Porter was a close observer of nature cannot be denied. The rigid training behind the camera contributed to a keenness of vision and a meticulous attention to detail. But her descriptions, although scientific in accuracy, do not read like "scientific" descriptions:

The clearest enunciator and the handsomest insect of all is the katy-did. . . . The adult is a solid green of pale color, yellowish in faint tints in some lights, a dainty bluish in others. The faceplate and wide "choker" appear to be of the same glassy coat of mail as those of the grasshopper. The legs are very long, and the hind pair has claspers. The wings resemble deeply veined and grooved leaves, the musical plates showing at the bases. The insect is very narrow of body, but quite deep, and the back and abdomen are sharp ridges. The antennae are almost twice the length of the body, and so hair-fine that a camera focused on a katy-did does not record their full extent. With these they explore their path, lightly touching objects before them to find footing and avoid danger. Their greatest protection lies in their close resemblance to tender green leaves.[27]

The idea of conservation prevails all through *Music of the Wild*, but nowhere more than in the section dealing with the "Songs of the Fields." Here Porter deplores the indiscriminate clearing of the forest to make farmland and the failure to leave enough of the trees and shrubs to nurture wildlife. She points out the value of the fencerow as a shelter for the birds so vital for the protection of crops. Of course, much of her interest and concern is aesthetic; she is as intent upon the preservation of beauty as she is upon the economic value of nature.

One of Porter's vexations was that too many "progressive" farmers not only cleared all nonagricultural vegetation from their farms but also from their homes. She grieved at farm houses standing isolated, ungraced, and unprotected by trees. She realized in a time of no energy crisis the insulating and air-conditioning value of trees surrounding a house. She lamented over farmsteads with barren yards and with stumps where trees had willfully been cut, leaving the house and yard shadeless.

"Songs of the Fields" concludes with a long account of and a tribute to the Limberlost. A fact unknown to readers of the novels is that "Limberlost" was, and is, the name of a creek and only incidentally the name of the swamp one corner of which it crosses. One is forced to wonder whether the story of the name—that of Limber being lost—is not apochryphal. Perhaps a truer interpretation would come from the meandering nature of the stream and its ability to lose itself in the impenetrable thickets of the forest or the spreading morasses of the swamp. Porter follows the course of this stream from where it "is born in the heart of swampy wood and thicket" to where it "flows through the upper corner of the old Limberlost swamp" and to where "a thing of beauty it goes laughing on the way to the Wabash."[28]

"The Music of the Marsh" answers the question, how does the swamp differ from the forest or the fields? The difference is water, either in running streams, deep pools, or spreading quagmire. And such a region has its own inhabitants which are not found elsewhere. There are, of course, many trees, shrubs, animals, birds, insects, and flowers which are common to all three locations. But there are water-loving trees—particularly the tamarack, the sycamore, and the willow; there are the innumerable water birds and the fish, frogs, turtles, and other water denizens; there are water animals—the muskrat, the otter, and the beaver; and there are the many plants which thrive only in the water or in the marsh surrounding it—the various water lilies, reeds and rushes, and the pitcher plants and ladies' slippers of the true bog.

Gene Stratton Porter reproduces with felicity the actual

sounds of the swamp—the frog chorus, the cries of the water birds, the buzzing of insects, the screams of hawk, eagle, or owl, and the numerous songs of the marsh birds—but she does much more. She records the passing of the swamp, the steady encroachment of man. "Although it is not so easy to attack the swamp as the forest, on all sides man is pressing close. Big ditches are being dredged, leading from the marshes lying highest on the face of the earth to lower bodies of running water, so that the marsh level is reduced by several feet, giving an unbelievable amount of space that soon dries out for cultivation."[29]

Gene Stratton Porter realized as did few in her time how the widespread destruction of forest and marshland could seriously affect the actual climate of a region. Long before the dust bowl of the depression years and before the water crises of the 1970s, she wrote of the permanent, irreversible changes in rainfall patterns resulting from the widespread and ruthless destruction of trees and swamps:

It was Thoreau who, in writing of the destruction of the forests, exclaimed, "Thank Heaven, they can not cut down the clouds!" Aye, but they can! That is a miserable fact, and soon it will become our discomfort and loss. Clouds are of vapor arising from damp places and floating in air until they meet other vapor masses, that mingle with them, and the weight becomes so great that the whole fall in drops of rain. If men in their greed cut forests that preserve and distil moisture, clear fields, take the shelter of trees from creeks and rivers until they evaporate, and drain the water from swamps so that they can be cleared and cultivated,—they *prevent vapor from rising;* and if it does not rise it can not fall. Pity of pities it is; but man can change and is changing the forces of nature. I never told a sadder truth, but it is truth that man can "cut down the clouds."[30]

There is neither space nor time to enumerate all the evidences of nature which present themselves in *Music of the Wild,* but the reader who wishes to become acquainted with the flora and fauna representative of the Midwest will find a wealth of material in this volume. Fortunately, Gene Stratton Porter was not entirely right in her prophecies of doom for her beloved wildlife, or perhaps her pleas for conservation bore fruit. At any rate, with a few exceptions, the birds, animals, trees, and flowers of which she wrote are still to be found although not in the same prodigality in which she knew them.

Tales You Won't Believe continues Gene Stratton Porter's account of her embracement of nature. Whether these nature books are more important as studies in natural history or as autobiography is hard to determine for, in addition to reporting the natural history around her, they are the story of her life—at least that part of it which was meaningful to her. Life history and natural history commingle in many passages:

Having spent my childhood in the country and being by six years the youngest of the family, I learned at an early age to amuse myself with the outdoors rather than in play with other children. So, from the earliest moment that I was allowed to wander at will, I made friends with the birds, with the flowers, with the trees, with anything and everything with which I came in contact. Perhaps my dearest playmates of all were three streams of running water that crossed our land. One of them, in the northern section of the land, was broad for a brook even in those days; shallow; and it had mucky banks where grew all kinds of sedges and swamp grasses, cat-tails and bulrushes, and great beds of blue flag. Willow trees grew on its banks in one shaggy patriarch of which a scarlet tanager nested almost every year, and the male bird, a thing of blood-red and coal-black colour, sang from the top branches and performed his share of tanager family life in near proximity to the flag bed which in bloom time was a sheet of blue that attracted both the wild and the domestic bees and the sweet-loving humming birds and the butterflies. In this same tree an oriole always swung its pendent purse of lint, plant fibre, and string ensuing from the dooryard. A thrilling riot of colour ensued when a bird of blood red and another of sun yellow began the activities of feeding two nests filled with clamouring young above a bed of blue wild iris beside a brook that threw rainbow shadows and had many secrets to whisper and sing and chuckle over. On all the land Father owned there was not a spot more exquisite than the small promontory on which grew the tanager and oriole willow, not even in the deep wood where the other small brook that ran from west to east passed the red flame of *Monarda didyma* and white violets climbed down the bank until they could see themselves in the water.[31]

Not unlike other Gene Stratton Porter nature books, *Tales You Won't Believe* was written as a series of magazine articles and first appeared in *Good Housekeeping* in fourteen issues extending from January 1924 through February 1925. To these story-essays was added another, "The Dog That I Saw Win Immunity," from the *Literary Digest*, when they were gathered together to make up the book.[32] The subject matter is all nature itself; Porter deals with birds, flowers, insects, and animals and the fascinating if not unbelievable experiences she has had with them. Her adventures were by no means usual. They range from herself becoming the best moth bait in the world, from her success in raising fringed gentians from seed, from her search for the rarest of native wild orchids, and from mysteriously disappearing wild white strawberries—all in Indiana—to her story of the dog who saved his master from a rattlesnake in Nebraska, and to a Memorial Day outing with her niece and grandniece at the home she was building in California.

As is to be expected, there is much in this volume that is repeated from earlier publications. The account of the wood duck is only slightly altered from that appearing in *Music of the Wild*. The story of the English skylarks occurs in *Homing with the Birds*, and the oriole's nest with the window is retold from several sources. But there is much that is new to this volume, and the entire book possesses a certain unity lacking in other books. perhaps because the original reading of each of the articles in *Good Housekeeping* would be separated from the others by a full month's span.

It may be that because this book was written late in the life of Gene Stratton Porter that it is more conservation oriented than any of the others. Throughout many of the essays there is told her struggle to save what she could of the vanishing wildlife of her region and to remove it to the safety of her own preserve. In the section "The Lost White Wild Strawberries" she tells of these efforts and of the laying out of "beds" of wildflowers, much like the spokes of a wheel, radiating from the Cabin, which was the hub. These beds were tracts of land of approximately an acre each, and in them she planted wildflowers according to color— red, white, pink, blue, and mauve. The last and largest bed surrounded the Cabin and was of what seems to have been her favorite color—yellow. It is puzzling as to why such an ardent nature lover as Gene Stratton Porter would attempt such a marshaling of colors, such an isolation, as occurs nowhere in nature.

Mrs. Porter considered the whole area of Northeastern Indiana, including the Limberlost, Sylvan Lake, and Wabash River localities, as her territory and as man and agriculture advanced upon it, she did what she could to save at least specimens of the vegetation that was being so rapidly destroyed.

In 1913 she had a corps of five trained men helping her in this effort. Many of the stories in *Tales You Won't Believe* are concerned with this struggle.

"The Last Passenger Pigeon" by its very title assures the reader that it is a conservation essay. And it is. But much of it is devoted to the changes that had occurred in her lifetime—to the indiscriminate cutting of the forests with the accompanying destruction of "uncounted millions of dollars in bird's eye maple, cherry, in burled oak, golden oak, black walnut, hickory, and the red elm so sought after now for knife handles and gun butts."[44] She tells of the diminution of all kinds of wildlife, and speaks specifically of the wanton killing of birds, animals, and fish far beyond the needs of the people. She tells of her last sight of a passenger pigeon and, in a passage sentimental but moving, she voices the condemnation by the bird of those who had all but exterminated it.

The bird might very well have been crying "See? See? See what you have done to me! See what you have done to your beautiful land! Where are your great stretches of forest? Where are the fish-thronged rivers your fathers enjoyed? Where are the bubbling springs and the sparkling brooks? Why is this land parching with thirst even in springtime? Why have you not saved the woods and the water and the wildflowers and the rustle of bird wings and the notes of their song? See what you have done to me! Where a few years ago I homed over your land in uncounted thousands, today I am alone. See me searching for a mate! See me hunting for a flock of my kind! See what you have done to me! See! See! See!"[34]

Tales you Won't Believe contains almost countless descriptions of scenes—of woods, swamp, meadows, roadsides, and shoreline. And in these settings Porter places the flowers and shrubs which grow and blossom there. But sometimes she is not conscientious of time. These scenes are recalled, not recorded, and her memories of her observations were not calendared. She had the rather annoying habit of compressing the seasons so that, for example, she has water lilies, blue flag, pickerel weed, cardinal flower, touch-me-not, wild roses, and alder [elder] all blooming at the same time and at a time which she establishes as being June. Actually, the cardinal flower and touch-me-not would not appear before late summer when most of the other flowers she names would be long gone. The same disregard in found in *The Harvester;* Ruth is painting mayapple and bloodroot along with the goldenseal and moonseed in the middle of September. The Harvester is digging roots, and Ruth may have been painting roots which are interesting in both shape and color in all the species, but the flowers are mentioned and the leaves which would have vanished long before September are described. Such lapses are rare rather than common in the nature writing of Gene Stratton Porter, and it is perhaps picayune to point them out. For the most part she observes and reports from the same point in time and portrays faithfully her environment.

In "The Search for 'Three Birds' " there is a long and detailed account of Porter's efforts to bring to her own premises the swamp growth threatened with extinction by a large drainage project in Noble County where Wildflower Woods is situated. She tells of her disbelief that such a scheme would be accomplished and points to its ecological dangers:

When I found that such a scheme had definitely gone through, that plans were being made that only the most stringent and immediate work could save Noble County, I was horrified. Drying up the springs, drying up the streams, and lowering the lake meant to exterminate the growth by running water, meant to kill the great trees which had flourished since the beginning of time around the borders of the lakes, meant to kill the vines and shrubs and bushes, the ferns and the iris and the water hyacinths, the arrowhead lilies and the rosemary and the orchids, and it meant, too, that men were madly and recklessly doing an insane thing without really understanding what they were doing. They had forgotten that where there is no moisture to arise to mass in clouds and fall back upon the earth, to be scattered in rain, no rain comes. They had forgotten that draining the water from all these acres of swamp land would dry and heat the air they were to breathe to an almost unendurable degree during summer. They had not studied the question scientifically and figured out for themselves how much rainfall they would take from their crops.[35]

Porter speaks of her efforts to fight the project and tells that she poured time and money into the battle, but she gives little detail. Instead she relates her own personal effort to save what she could from devastation: "Life became one round of fight. Fight from morning till night. Fight for the war, fight for the conservation of physical and spiritual comfort and of hunt, seek, and search to rescue every one of these delicate little blossoms possible before destruction overtook them."[36]

One can but commend Gene Stratton Porter for her efforts to enlist the support of the public in the preservation and conservation of natural resources—soil, water, woodland, and wildlife. Her own life had ended before the last magazine series was completed and before the last book was published. But the contribution that Mrs. Porter made to the movement for nature study in the schools and for conservation all over the land can hardly be overestimated.

CHAPTER 5

The Right Writer for Her Time

I The Time itself

THE writing of Gene Stratton Porter spans the first quarter of the twentieth century. Her work began in 1900 with the series of magazine articles in *Recreation,* and her death occurred in 1924. There were posthumous publications, but the final publication of anything written by Gene Stratton Porter was the collection of essays, *Let Us Highly Resolve,* in 1927. (This book was published in August but the final editorial in the *McCall's* series did not appear until December.) By the succeeding decade, the enormous popularity of Mrs. Porter's novels and somewhat less popular nature books was on the decline. True, the sales of her books continued, and still continues, but the numbers were by no means comparable to the staggering sales of the early years. Her novels still circulate well from the shelves of public libraries, and there is an increasing interest in her nature books.

It is useless to speculate as to whether Gene Stratton Porter more or less fortuitously appeared on the scene at just the right time to assure her popularity or whether the times shaped her and made her the right writer for the period. Whatever the cause, Porter came before a reading audience that was ripe and ready for her. It was a reading public which wanted sentiment and romance but which was willing to accept something more— the deep look into the wonders of nature which Porter could provide. It was this added something which made Porter popular.

Gene Stratton Porter, like many of her contemporaries, grew up in the immediate post-Civil War North. During her formative years, America was experiencing the rapid growth of industry and big business. The accumulation of great fortunes that

117

accompanied such growth was in progress. Immigration was at a
high point, and the movement from the farm to the city was at a
new height. But, as is made clear in the pages of *Michael
O'Halloran,* the flight to suburbia was already beginning.

The aftermath of the Civil War left the country solidly
Republican until the election of Grover Cleveland in 1884. The
Strattons had always been as staunchly Republican as the
majority of the rest of the country and had worked hard for the
party, and the Democratic victory was a blow to them. A mob of
celebrants attacked their house in Wabash and "with long-
brooms swept our residence from the upper story to the lower.
Regardless of flower beds and the lawn, they rode around us, a
howling mob, for my father had always had the courage of his
convictions. He had made many speeches; he had always
influenced many voters. That day he sat in his residence with his
head bowed and his heart almost broken; then we waited in fear
and trembling to learn what the awful Democrats were going to
do."[1] Fortunately, the country and the Strattons survived the
Democratic victory.

But there were changes other than political. The full impact of
the Industrial Revolution was not felt in the United States until
after 1870. The almost explosive expansion of railroads, steel,
and oil led to the dominant industrialization of America and
turned it away from a primarily agrarian economy toward the era
of big manufacturing and big business. Hungry machines and
commerce drew people away from the farms and into the cities.
But the indigent population was not sufficient to supply the need
for labor, and the great waves of immigration surged. Between
1870 and 1900, the population of the United States doubled,
reaching 76 million by the turn of the century.[2]

The most important influxes of people were from European
countries and were added to the growing density of population
on the eastern seaboard. But there was also immigration across
the Pacific; the western railroads were built for a great part with
Chinese labor, and Chinese and other Oriental "towns" grew up
in the West Coast cities of San Francisco, Los Angeles, Portland,
and Seattle. And among the flood of immigrants there were many
who were of the land and saw in America the opportunity to
become farmers, not peasants. Many of these people contributed
to the settlement of Gene Stratton Porter's section of Indiana
and, incidentally, to the wholesale destruction of forest and

swamp which she was to deplore. Many more paused with the hospitable Strattons on their way farther west.[3] The dream, even the expectation, that hard work would result in riches, flourished in the early years of the century and resulted in the transplanting of almost nine million Americans in the decade of from 1900 to 1910. Gene Stratton Porter was to find many of her most loyal readers in the followers of the great American dream.

The early years of the twentieth century saw an acceleration of the concentration of the population in a relatively few immense cities spread across the land: New York, Philadelphia, and Boston in the East; Chicago, Milwaukee, and St. Louis in middle America; and Los Angeles and San Francisco on the West Coast. The move to the cities had begun by 1890, but 8 million farm workers still outnumbered those in all other industries. In 1900, only a fourth of 76 million Americans lived in towns of 25,000 or over, but the 1920 census revealed more people in cities and towns than on farms or in villages of less than 25,000. In the millions of recently uprooted citizenry who remembered or perhaps longed for the rural lives they had led, Porter found an eager and appreciative readership.

The Spanish War was over, and the dominant political figure to emerge from it was the dynamic Theodore Roosevelt. But, in addition to being a political figure and perhaps a statesman, Roosevelt was also an ardent wildlife enthusiast and a conservationist. His enthusiasm and his writing did much to awaken the interest of the American people in nature and to make the soil ripe for the tilling of Gene Stratton Porter. The President and the nature lover were mutual admirers, so much so that Mrs. Porter and Jeannette were invited to spend an afternoon with the President at Sagamore, his estate on Long Island.[4] This experience is no doubt reflected in the descriptions of Long Island mansions in *The Magic Garden,* for Gene Stratton Porter was a keen observer, and what she saw she remembered, and what she remembered she employed.

The great concerns of the urbanization of America were of little or no consequence to Gene Stratton Porter; she had no real knowledge of them. Isolated in what can truthfuly be described as a backward area in Indiana, she was at least in the early part of her writing career—but dimly aware of the great movements shaping the country. The struggle of labor for recognition as an equal partner with capital in the development of industry, the great spiral of deflation following the Spanish War, with its attendant questions of free silver or the "Crucifixion of Mankind upon a Cross of Gold," the Populist and Agrarian movements—of these she read in the newspaper, but they were something remote, not immediate to her. Not being familiar with the great cities, she did not realize the horrors of overcrowding in slums and tenements, and her use of city scenes in her novels—especially in *Michael O'Halloran*—is from the viewpoint of a casual observer, not that of one thoroughly familiar with the scene. The tenement room shared by Mickey and Lily Peaches is nestlike, almost pleasant.

Mrs. Porter was aware of the movement for women's rights, but she was by no means a suffragette. She was willing for women to have the *right* to vote, but she thought they should be governed by their husbands in exercising this right.[5] Woman's place—contrary to her own activity—was in the home, and for most women it took all of their time and energy to be a proper home-maker. Of course, there were exceptions; if there were no husband, or if he were utterly dissolute, then the woman must be both breadwinner and home-maker. But the opportunities for women in the novels of Gene Stratton Porter were few. They could teach school, they could do fine needlework—engaging in millinery or dressmaking—or they could do artwork for illustration and design. Elnora Comstock in *A Girl of the Limberlost* does earn money by reaping nature, and there is at least a suggestion that women as well as men might follow the methods of the Harvester. But only Kate Bates in *A Daughter of the Land* and Marian Thorne in *Her Father's Daughter* encroach upon the men's world, Kate by becoming a farmer and Marian, an architect. Linda Strong, her father's daughter, becomes a writer of recipes.

None of her heroines exercises the women's rights which Gene Stratton Porter exhibited in her own life. But, in all fairness, Porter insisted that her first duties were those of housekeeper and mother. And again in all fairness, it must be pointed out that when she left the rather masculine world in which her fieldwork was done, she shed—with her mannish costume—any mannish ways she may have had and became the essence of femininity in her own home and in the social circles in which she moved. She had a fondness for fine clothes, for rich fabrics, and for articles of personal adornment. She was especially fond of elaborate fans.[6]

Those Americans who succumbed to the lure of the big cities felt nostalgic about the home town or the farm they had left behind. In spite of being caught up in the stresses of city life, they had a yearning for the farm and small-town normalcy of former years. As people turned away from the overcrowded and restless cities and looked backward to a more peaceful, rich, and enduring—though physically difficult—life, where the family was the main institution, they often felt the need to establish such ties as possible with this past. Gene Stratton Porter brought to her times all the simple goodness, the warmth, the neighborliness, and the kindness for which millions of Americans yearned. Rural folk clung to the old-fashioned virtues, and new city folk longed for a return to them.

Another facet of the expanding twentieth century that contributed to the popularity of Gene Stratton Porter was the great proliferation of women's magazines. There were many of them, some with small circulation, some with large, but most prominent among them—and the ones to which Porter contributed most frequently—were the *Ladies' Home Journal, Good Housekeeping,* and *McCall's* all of which are alive and thriving today. Others like the *Delineator,* the *Woman's Home Companion,* and the *Pictorial Review* have passed into oblivion, although not necessarily because they failed to print Porter—the *Delineator* was graced with an appearance or two. The prime, but by no means the sole, readership of these magazines was the great body of middle-class American housewives. They read for pleasure, and they read for escape, and Gene Stratton Porter was able to supply them with both at one time. Pehaps when it came to the long series of articles or editorials appearing in *McCall's* under the heading, "Gene Stratton-Porter's Page," the women read for enlightenment, but it was still pleasurable reading, and the material reinforced the ideas and ideals of the popular culture. In the January issue of *McCall's* for 1922, in one of her early articles, Porter herself saluted the women's magazines for the good work they were doing. She singled out the same three—the *Ladies' Home Journal, Good Housekeeping,* and *McCall's*—as being the leaders in the field.

The first World War intervened almost in the middle of the career of Gene Stratton Porter. Again, she was an observer rather than a participant; the war was somewhat remote from the Limberlost. She suffered the privations of shortages and prices; she made her contribution to the war effort in saving, knitting, and preserving; she suffered for the sons of friends and members of her own family, including her driver, who were in army or navy; but her encounter with the war was second-hand, through newspapers and magazines of the day and from her voluminous correspondence—many of her letters were from "the boys overseas." While the war had little or no effect on the writing or natural history work of Porter, it had a most intensifying effect on the forces that shaped her audience. The entire populace became more mobile, and more and more of the nation's youth left the farm never to return. But to the trenches and to "No Man's Land" they took with them *Freckles* and *A Girl of the Limberlost* for the escape they offered from the horrors of conflict. And when they returned, if they returned, they still read Gene Stratton Porter.[7]

With the end of the war came an acceleration of the pace of American cosmopolitanism and urbanization. Life moved swiftly—too swiftly—and the old values seemed lost in the excesses and moral breakdown of prohibition and the jazz decade. But the trend away from the old values and the old morality was by no means universal. The Eighteenth Amendment was not foisted upon the nation by an articulate minority, however helpful that minority may have been. Evangelists and evangelism flourished, as witness Billy Sunday and Aimee Semple McPherson. The old order yielded somewhat, but not without a struggle. Indeed, the old moral code was never completely obliterated—it lurked beneath the surface—and there are many still adhering, at least to some extent, to it today. And there were those who still clung to the old literary tastes which governed the first quarter of the century. Realism and Naturalism might flourish, but there were still those who preferred sentiment and romance.

II *Popularity and Best-Sellerism*

"If piled on top of one another, Mrs. Gene Stratton-Porter's books would reach a height of 1,250,000 feet or 1600 times the height of the Woolworth Building."[8] So wrote Eugene Saxton in 1915. It is quite an impressive statistic today when the stack would merely be equal to 966 World Trade Centers or 916 Sears Towers. And 1915 was only the halfway point in the career of

Gene Stratton Porter. She had published thirteen books by this time (not counting the curious little *Birds of the Limberlost*) and thirteen more were to follow. Of course, none of the final thirteen ever achieved the same popularity as did *Freckles, A Girl of the Limberlost, The Harvester,* and *Laddie;* still, *Her Father's Daughter, The White Flag,* and *The Keeper of the Bees* had highly respectable sales, and the final tower would indeed be impressive.

Gene Stratton Porter was one of the best-selling writers of the first quarter of the twentieth century. In fact, if one discounts paperback and book-club publication, which were not popular in her day, Porter still ranks among the top ten American best-sellers.[9] Suzanne Greene states that "a top best seller is defined as any book which, during its total life, has sold a number of copies equal to one per cent of the population of the United States at the beginning of the decade in which it was first issued."[10] A best-seller is obviously any book that sells more copies than other books in a given time period. It is a reflection not necessarily of the best books but of the books people have liked best or which they have purchased for some reason or other. A best-seller differs from a literary classic in that the latter continues to be read and to be appreciated by succeeding generations of readers. There are weekly, monthly, and annual best-seller lists, and an appearance on any one or all three of these does not necessarily guarantee top best-sellerism.[11]

For example, *Freckles,* with an all-time sales record of 2,809,523, and *A Girl of the Limberlost,* with 2,053,892, never appeared on any annual best-seller list. *The Harvester,* with only 1,611,007 copies sold, appeared on two such lists. It was in fifth place in 1911 and rose to first place in 1912. *Laddie* and *Michael O'Halloran,* which closely followed *The Harvester* in sales, were each in third place in 1913 and 1915 respectively. *A Daughter of the Land, Her Father's Daughter,* and *The Keeper of the Bees* all rated a place on the annual lists but failed to reach the magic of top best-sellerism. *The White Flag,* in spite of its having had the greatest prepublication sale of any book in history up to its time, never reached one of the annual lists, although it had quite significant sales.[12] Perhaps the serialization of the book in *Good Housekeeping* hurt the sales of the hardcover book; however, The *Keeper of the Bees* reached third place in 1925 in spite of its almost simultaneous serialization in *McCall's.*

With the publication of *Michael O'Halloran* in 1915, Gene Stratton Porter had achieved five commanding top best-sellers. In American sales up to this time only Charles Dickens and Sir Walter Scott had listed more titles. Mark Twain, Rudyard Kipling, and Mrs. E. D. E. N. Southworth had four each. But Harold Bell Wright was soon to match Porter.[13] It has been estimated that during her lifetime Mrs. Porter earned more than two million dollars from the sale of her ten novels, seven nature books, and two each of children's books and poetry, with the novels accounting for the bulk of her sales.[14] And there were yet to come two novels, a nature book, and a collection of essays—all issued after her death.

The mere listing of the publications of Gene Stratton Porter, including different editions of the books, foreign translations, and magazine articles, but excluding newspaper publication and motion picture scenarios, totals over six hundred items.[15] Her output is breathtaking in sheer numbers. Part of this popularity was due to the intense interest in fiction during the early years of the century. As Tebbel puts it, "Between 1890 and the First World War, the reading of fiction in America became something of a mania, novels were devoured as much as read, and the public appetite appeared to be insatiable. Advertising budgets reflected this phenomenon; most houses used about 70% of them for fiction. At the thick of this craze, novels by writers like Harold Bell Wright and Gene Stratton Porter enjoyed hardcover sales in the hundreds of thousands for each title."[16]

Reading habits are not recorded in sales records alone. No popular book (or classical book, for that matter) represents one group of readers compared or contrasted with another group. There is a great overlap among books and readers. Readers who read Gene Stratton Porter were also probably reading Ellen Glasgow, Edith Wharton, and Sinclair Lewis—perhaps even Theodore Dreiser and Willa Cather. Bernard Berelson writes that "it is known that from ten to twenty percent of the adult book readers do seventy percent of the reading."[17] Thus, there is a great group of constant readers as opposed to an even greater group of occasional readers. Berelson's figures were for 1951; there would have been even more overlap in the first quarter of the century because motion pictures were rare, radio not yet widespread, and television unknown. Travel was somewhat difficult; the great age of the automobile with its accompanying web of highways had not arrived. People stayed at home more. More time was devoted to reading, and people read more books.

The sales records of books by no means delineates the number of readers. How many persons read each copy sold, either as family members or borrowers? It is an unanswerable question, as obviously no pertinent records exist. How many persons read these titlles in circulating libraries? Again, no accurate figures are available, but Irving Hart states that "for the period 1919 to 1931 an 80% correlation has been found to exist between the bookstore best sellers and books with the highest library circulation."[18]

To this already impressive readership must be added those who read Gene Stratton Porter in the magazines exclusively. The devotees of "Gene Stratton-Porter's Page" in *McCall's* were legion, and much of the nature writing appeared first in periodicals. The novels *The White Flag, The Keeper of the Bees,* and *The Magic Garden* were serialized as was the long poem *Euphorbia.* It becomes quite apparent that the claim of "the life that touched fifty million lives" was no idle boast. It is interesting to note that Porter was published consistently and simultaneously in two of the leading "ladies' magazines," *McCall's* and *Good Housekeeping.* For five years no issue of *McCall's* failed to carry at least one Porter item; often there were two, as when a novel was being serialized or the poem *Whitmore's Bull* was being printed, or even three, as in the October 1927 issue which contained, in addition to the regular page, two little sketches of New York. But during these five years there were twenty-six months in which Gene Stratton Porter was also in *Good Housekeeping.*

The time of Gene Stratton Porter's greatest popularity encompassed the First World War and the turmoil both preceding and following it. Yet, as has been noted, Porter did not write of the war. But she was not alone. The writers and the readers of the popular front seemed oblivious to the approaching conflict. None of the best selling books of 1913-14 even remotely suggested the imminence or the actuality of war in Europe. "In 1913, the year before the outbreak of the first World War in Europe, the mood of Americans was implicit in what they were reading: Harrison's *V V's Eyes,* Churchill's *Inside the Cup,* Frances Hodgson Burnett's *T Tembaroom,* Gene Stratton-Porter's *Laddie,* Eleanor H. Porter's *Pollyanna,* Maeterlinck's

Our Eternity, Arnold Bennett's *Paris Nights.* These romantic, sentimental, family books were followed in 1914 by Booth Tarkington's *Penrod,* Theodore Roosevelt's *Autobiography,* and John Fox's *The Heart of the Hills.*"[19]

It was the poets rather than the novelists who interpreted the conflict while the war was in progress; "In Flanders' Fields" and "The Soldier" were immensely popular. Dorothy Canfield Fisher's *Home Fires in France* and John Dos Passos's *Three Soldiers,* both in 1918, went practically unnoticed except by critics. Laurence Stallings in *What Price Glory?* (with Maxwell Anderson) in 1924 and *The Big Parade* in 1925 had attacked the war from the stage, but it was not until *All Quiet on the Western Front* and *A Farewell to Arms,* both in 1929, that the great mass of American readers began to accept war novels. *The Sun Also Rises* (1926) gained its greatest readership after *A Farewell to Arms* had become popular.

At least a part of the explanation of the popularity of Gene Stratton Porter as author must be attributed to her choice of publishers. The unquestioned leading house of the time was Doubleday, Page & Company. Porter's first work to see original publication with this firm was *Freckles* in 1904, and after 1912 all her books bore the Doubleday, Page imprint. The leadership of this firm was in great part due to the dynamism of its leader, Mr. F. N. Doubleday, who, wisely enough, took an active personal as well as business interest in his string of writers. Mr. Doubleday had many best-selling authors on his book list. In addition to Porter, there were Edna Ferber, Ellen Glasgow, O. Henry, Sinclair Lewis, Kathleen Norris, and Booth Tarkington among others. Moreover, he was the American publisher for his good English friends Rudyard Kipling, Joseph Conrad, Ramsay Mac-Donald, and T. E. Lawrence.[20]

Essentially it is sales that make a publishing house successful, and it is sales that make a writer wealthy. The novels of Gene Stratton Porter sold by the millions in the early years of the twentieth century, both in the regular editions put out by Doubleday, Page and in the popular (and cheaper) issues of Grosset and Dunlap. The relationship between author and publisher was mutually advantageous; Porter became financially independent, and Doubleday, Page, with an eye to profit, did all it could through advertising and publicity to promote the sale of her books. Gene Stratton Porter profited, too; the efforts of her publishers did much to establish her popularity, to capture her readers—to make them receptive to nature books as well as novels—and to insure the faithful following of the millions who awaited each new Porter offering with eager anticipation.

The popular culture of America is at least as worthy of consideration in the history of letters as is the culture of the intelligentsia. It would perhaps have been a fine thing if readers of the first quarter of the twentieth century had read Theodore Dreiser and Willa Cather with the same avidity with which they read Harold Bell Wright and Gene Stratton Porter. It would perhaps have been a fine thing if people of the next five decades had read William Faulkner and Flannery O'Connor instead of Mickey Spillane and Grace Metalious. But they did not. If the concern is reading rather than Literature, the latter writers in each period cannot be ignored.

III *Critics and Criticism*

Gene Stratton Porter was neither of nor for the intelligentsia. She wrote for the masses, for the millions who got their pleasures vicariously from the romances of the popular magazines. Her audience was for the most part feminine, middle class, and traditionally minded; it was idealistic, hopeful, and cheerful. Her novels offered an escape from the pettiness of life. In them one could forget the drudgery of everyday existence; in them one could go back and reexperience (or experience for the first time) the beauty and simplicity of nature. And it was this deep and abiding love for nature and her mission to instill a like response in her readers which most critics fail to understand. She attempted to make it clear enough: "Personally, I never had the nerve to call a book that I wrote 'a novel' or expected that it should be judged on a fictional basis. I never have understood why my books should be put in the same category as the realistic novel, since they are as different as day from night in intention, execution, and results."[21]

But her books were put into the category of novels and were subjected to criticism as novels, and with mixed results. They fared badly indeed at the hands of campus critics and the intelligentsia in general. But, as R. Baird Shuman points out, "Contemporary critical judgments about artists of all kinds have been notoriously short-sighted and patently incorrect. Throughout history. . .critics have made poorly supported and dimly illuminated judgments."[22]

And so it was with Porter. Neither the critics who were for her nor those against her rendered a fair evaluation; the former were overebullient in their praise, the latter too harsh in their condemnation. Until very recently pedantic critics writing of American literature have either ignored Gene Stratton Porter completely or have denigrated her as a cheap, money-grubbing sentimentalist. Perhaps she was not a great novelist, but neither was she an insincere hack.

It may be that some of Porter's success was due to the fact that there were editors and critics still around who were gentlemen of the old school, in other words who were attuned to the times—the same times that made Gene Stratton Porter and her audience not only possible but inevitable. Among these editors were Perriton Maxwell of *Metropolitan*, Richard Watson Gilder of *Century*, and at a little later date Edward W. Bok of the *Ladies' Home Journal.* Among those critics who spoke favorably in review of her work were William Lyon Phelps, Charles Wharton Stork, and Orrin Root, to be joined later by Christopher Morley.

That some of her contemporary reviewers went a little far cannot be denied. One of them in writing of *The Song of the Cardinal* declared:

This exquisite contribution to the rapidly growing literature dealing with Nature studies and forest lore deserves a place in every American home. It will do for the birds of the forest what "Black Beauty" did for the horse. We cannot conceive of a boy or girl, or one of older years, who has read its pages, ever again being able to wantonly slaughter the feathered singers of forest and field. It will awaken the tender and essentially noble emotions which inspire a reverence for life and a sympathetic and loving interest in Nature, in a way that cannot fail to enrich the character of its readers. . . .

The story is admirably told from first to last, and there are many passages of great beauty. The descriptions are especially vivid, while the excellent reproductions of photographs taken by the author add much to the interest of the volume, which is handsomely printed and will make a beautiful and appropriate presentation work. If the Audubon Society should circulate thousands of copies of this work, it would do far more to revolutionize public sentiment than the expenditure of the same amount of money in dry arguments or heated protests.[23]

But unstinted praise was countered by such comments as, "Minute nature study is, with this author, not so much a fad as a fanaticism, and the scientific value of her labors is largely discounted by the open and unabashed self-satisfaction of her style. Even more plainly can her foibles and shortcomings be seen in *The Song of the Cardinal,* her first attempt at anything approaching fiction,—although, in spite of the introduction of two or three human beings, it is really the story of a pair of Cardinal birds, and distinctly, albeit unconsciously of the nature-faking sort."[24] The critic continues and rather grudgingly admits that the writing has some value and then sinks his barb again: ". . .It has been generally conceded that their interest lies, not in the story, but in the background and atmosphere, in the sense of outdoor life and sunshine and the sheer jubilant joy of living. In point of fact, she does sometimes achieve these effects, even though at times she inclines toward verboseness and redundancy, and there is a cloying sweetness in her nature worship that puts a matter-of-fact reader somewhat out of patience."[25]

The same disparity of judgment is found in criticism of *The Keeper of the Bees* published in the year after Gene Stratton Porter's death. Two New York papers published on the same day reviews of the book, the first of which stated that "A sense of sincerity shines through its pages. Mrs. Stratton-Porter wrote as she did because she felt what she was saying and believed it thoroughly. She has packed it full of cheery optimism, her homely wisdom, her love of fields and flowers and her own abundant and abiding faith."[26] But the other paper found the novel ". . .distinctly second rate, relieved only by its evident sincerity. There is faith in the fiction of Mrs. Stratton-Porter and faith is a keel to the craft of any one's adventure."[27] At least these critics agree as to the quality of faith being in the novel.

If one considers Porter's literary importance from the point of view of professional (and pehaps pedantic) critics, she fares badly indeed. But in considering literary importance one must immediately question, importance to whom? The mere fact that she pleased and satisfied literally millions of readers assures her a kind of literary importance which cannot be denied. There are critics who seem to think that small circulation is usually a sign of peculiar merit, and they are usually wrong. Popularity has to be achieved; it is not something the budding author labors to escape. After all, Willa Cather, Edith Wharton, and Ellen

Glasgow were as popular in their own days as at present. One fact that critics often ignore is that it is ultimately the reader who decides whether or not a piece of writing is literature.

When enough time had elapsed that critics could look back upon the first quarter of the twentieth century as historical, Mrs. Porter was almost entirely overlooked or was viewed disparagingly. Carl Van Doren wrote of the "domestic sentimentalism of Gene Stratton-Porter who piled sentimentalism upon descriptions of nature in soft sweet heaps," and went on to say that "she throbbed with all the current impulses, was popular with the uncritical multitude, and exhibited the rosy empty features of banality."[28] It rather seems that Van Doren is striking an attitude rather than attempting a careful analysis of Porter's work.

Grant Overton, a critic writing while Gene Stratton Porter was still alive, was kinder to her. He compared her rather favorably with Theodore Roosevelt and saw that her "edited and published fiction is of itself remarkable for an unrestraint, a vigorous emphasis, a masculine feel with which there is generally combined freshness of feeling and a transparent sincerity." He admired her "kind of self-sufficiency" and her "capacity that could have overcome mountains and found only moderately difficult hills in her path."[29]

Russell Nye, looking backward from 1970 at Gene Stratton Porter and her time, saw her as one of the "glad" writers along with Grace Livingston Hill, Eleanor H. Porter, and Kate Douglas Wiggin. But he recognized that Porter possessed qualities that the others lacked. In addition to her cheerfulness, she could tell a story—particularly a love story—and she could profit from the currently popular outdoor school of Muir, Burroughs, Seton, and Roosevelt and make nature-loving sentimentality her hallmark. The formula she developed was a good one. Nye says that it consisted of "sentimentality, faith and optimism, innocence and trust, nostalgia for country life, the curative and educational powers of Nature (with a capital N)."[30]

The rather staid *Literary History of the United States,* perhaps in an attempt to "bridge the gap between university scholarship and the interests of the educated public" admits that "by 1910 there was in fact a larger public for books than would exist for many years after the First World War. . . . It liked novels chiefly; it liked them if they were full of sentiment or swordplay, adventures in far places or local color; and if, at the same time, they moved by resolute steps toward an ending that satisfied the Protestant conventions. It liked Gene Stratton Porter, who by 1915 had written *Freckles* and four other novels with a total sale of eight million copies."[31] Porter's novels fit into all the categories; they are full of sentiment and swing along scene by scene, the Limberlost was remote enough from the rest of the country to fit "adventures in far places," and in *Freckles* at least there is certainly gunplay if not swordplay.

Mrs. Porter was not one to fail to take arms against a sea of critics even if she could not by opposing end them. Her complaint was that critics were judging her harshly because they did not understand her, did not comprehend what she was trying to do. She wanted her books to be judged as nature works, not as novels. She supplied just enough fiction to interest and carry along her readers so that they would tolerate (and absorb) her message, which was that lives can be enriched through contact with nature. Whether or not she was right in this position, it cannot be denied that her critics were not of her world—almost by deninition, critics are citydwellers.

In the article Mrs. Porter wrote in 1916 for the London *Bookman* introducing herself to her new English readers (eleven of her titles were being published in England for the first time), she took issue with some of her critics—those who saw her as a money-grubber, living a life of ease, and unacquainted with the milieu of her books. She pointed out that she could make much more money by abandoning nature and writing straight fiction, and that her field work in woods and swamp was far from a life of ease.[32]

Porter was particularly incensed by an article "by a man who does not deserve the prominence the mention of his name would give him." This man, however, was Frederick Taber Cooper, and the article was the one from which Cooper's criticism of *The Song of the Cardinal* has been quoted earlier. She took specific exception to being called a "nature-faker" and to the statement that "the scientific value of her labor is largely discounted by the open and unabashed self-satisfaction of her style."

This was a blow that hurt; her whole life had been devoted to the observation and reporting of nature, and while perhaps she at times had a tendency to humanize and to sentimentalize a little too much, her observations were in-depth and her

reporting accurate to the extreme. She was disgusted that
Cooper would stoop to falsifying a quotation from *The Song of
the Cardinal* (which he did) to prove his point of nature-faking.
As Cooper put it, "At times her imagery is unconsciously
grotesque, as when she tells us that the female bird 'blushed with
embarrassment to a colour even brighter than her natural
red!' "[33] Porter was right; the quotation does not appear
anywhere in *The Song of the Cardinal*. She is quick to point out
that the female cardinal is gray, not red, and that she who had
watched birds all her life would be the last to attribute a blush to
a feathered creature.

There is no doubt that adverse criticism hurt Porter just as
much as she reveled in favorable comments. Yet she was able to
select to herself criticism which pleased her and ignore (in the
same article) that which did not. In a letter to William Lyon
Phelps she says, "I was pathetically grateful to you for what
appeared to me to be something approaching adequate recognition of a lifetime of scientific field work."[34] But the article to
which she referred dealt with *A Daughter of the Land* and *A
Girl of the Limberlost*, the first of which Phelps admired greatly
while the second, he could not abide.[35]

Almost all the critics of her time, whether friendly or
unfriendly, had to admit however grudgingly that the work of
Gene Stratton Porter was interesting, that it was sincere, and
that she possessed to a rare degree that natural ability to tell a
story. Again quoting from William Lyon Phelps who, by the way,
must be classed among the friendly critics, "I defy any
unprejudiced person to read 'A Daughter of the Land' to the
end, without enthusiasm for the story. The style is so crude that
one must determine not to be stopped by it; one must not quit.
Apart from the lack of stylistic art, one will find an admirable
story, with a real plot and real characters; nothing is shirked or
softened in the course of the novel, and the heroine is a girl that
holds one's attention, not merely by what happens to her, but by
what she is."[36]

Much of the adverse criticism which was directed against
Gene Stratton Porter was really directed against that class of
writers to whom, admittedly, she belonged—those who wrote
for the popular audience. The critics were prone to dismiss
Porter along with the others without giving her the closer look
she deserved. For her novels do not quite fit into the pattern of

those others. While built on the somewhat commonplace theme of triumph over adversity, while developing uncomplicated plots, and while stressing the unfashionable values of goodness and honesty, they still have a depth and an intensity which others lack.

Many of her critics viewed Gene Stratton Porter's use of nature for background as a detriment to her novels—something to be tolerated for the sake of the story. Others, who perhaps came nearer to the truth of the matter, saw that it was the use of nature which was almost solely Porter's own possession which lent extra value to her work. Besides being nature-informing and pleasant to read they displayed a "vigorous personality and genuine enthusiasm which made [them] beloved by thousands who would never read Muir and would find Thoreau incomprehensible and alien."[37]

CHAPTER 6

As the Years Go By

I An Evaluation

A S the years go by there comes a time for the last part of the century to take a new look at the first part, to reevaluate it in terms of new understandings and new perspectives. Removed from the rebellion against the old order which marked the middle years, perhaps the time is ripe for a new look at Gene Stratton Porter and her books.

The novels of Gene Stratton Porter are not as bad as those critics who deign to mention her at all in the history of American literature would lead one to believe. It cannot be denied that she mistook popularity for worth. She points in many instances to the statistics of the sales of her books as evidence of their greatness. She wrote, "I have done every one of my books from my heart's best impulse, made them as clean and decent as I know how, and as beautiful and as interesting."[1] But she failed to recognize or to accept the fact that the appeal of her books lay not primarily in their cleanliness, their decency, or even in their beauty, but in the truth that they were interesting. For it is true that Porter possessed the rare quality of being able to arouse and sustain the interest of her readers through the most transparent of plots, the most obvious resolvement of situations, and the most advantageous workings of circumstance. The readers of her day were more willing to accept her "good" people leading their "good" lives (or suffering the consequences) than are the readers of today because her morality was somewhat closely attuned to the ideal morality of the time. But the modern reader who by some quirk of fortune picks up a Porter book for "idle reading on a summer's day" is likely to be gripped and carried along by the genuine interest of her story. Perhaps this fact accounts for the appeal that Porter novels still have for adolescent readers.

Porter made much of the fact that her stories were real; that her characters and incidents were drawn from life as she had lived it and knew it; that her stories were shared emotional experiences. She seemed unaware of Nietzsche's doctrine that no true artist tolerates reality. Yet, as Mrs. Porter builds scene on scene, her novels gain a certain intensity; they have a sense of the theatrical. It is no happenstance that Porter the photographer uses the photographic or scenic method in many passages of her novels. Even her descriptive passages are *composed* as if glimpsed through a view finder. It was this same quality which led to her ability to translate her novels into scenarios for the motion picture screen.

There are many minuses encountered in considering the works of Gene Stratton Porter, but there are also many pluses. Her works do lend themselves to criticism because of the limited depth of her characterizations; often cardboard characters lacking in scope people her stories. Her narratives are formula fixed, and her plots are self-evident. But it is not quite all true. The interest in the novels stems certainly not from curiosity; one knows unerringly what is going to happen, but one is intrigued by how it is going to happen. One element of this interest is that her characters are not as simply drawn as they seem; they behave in unexpected rather than expected ways. Many of Porter's women act quite unconventionally for women of her day. Jane Bakerman has drawn a comparison between Elnora of *A Girl of the Limberlost* and the Swamp Angel of *Freckles* and finds "a surprisingly refreshing dimension in her heroines," and, Bakerman continues, "Both young women, Elnora Comstock and the Angel are tough young women. This toughmindedness is used in a variety of ways, but each contributes to the sensationalism of the book—both intentionally and unwittingly."[2]

Elnora's mother, Kate Comstock, is herself a study in contradictions, and it is these contradictions which make her an interesting character—perhaps the most finely drawn that Porter ever created. Her scathing denunciation of Elvira Carney (the woman with whom her husband had been unfaithful, and which infidelity led to his death) is followed immediately by her rejection of Elvira's cancer as retribution for her sin and by her suggestion of a remedy which Elvira could use to relieve her pain. The contradiction is heightened by the fact that Kate was obsessed in her grief to the point that she had grown habitually harsh in her treatment of Elnora and could only occasionally allow the deep love she actually felt for her daughter to express itself, at first gradually, but later increasingly.

Some characters in Porter books are as unpredictable as others are predictable. Often characters fail to react as they obviously should react in a given situation. The stubborn refusal of Ruth to accept all David Langston offers her seems unreal (*The Harvester*). Kate Bates seems almost blind in her inability to see the transparently right course of action she should take (*A Daughter of the Land*). Mickey's "adoption" of Lily Peaches is not the behavior one would expect from a tough, battling, city news urchin (*Michael O'Halloran*). Jamie MacFarlane must have been highly insensate not to see how he was being used by the Storm Girl (*The Keeper of the Bees*). And it is this uncertainty as to whether a character will react as the reader expects him to react that maintains the interest in a Porter book.

While a great deal of the imagery in the novels is admittedly shopworn by today's standards, it must be remembered that the writing is now well over a half century old; perhaps a degree of the triteness may be attributed to the passage of time and the use and reuse of what was somewhat more original when Porter wrote it. Even a cursory examination of newspapers, books, and periodicals of the time shows that such rather florid writing was highly popular.

Hamilton W. Mabie once congratulated William Dean Howells for his clean heart and genuine purity, but as Van Wyck Brooks noted, he ignored Howells's primly virtuous attitudes and ignored also the vast exclusions the possession of those traits in a novelist implied.[3] But the novels of Gene Stratton Porter, in spite of her protestations as to their cleanliness and purity, are revealed, upon closer scrutiny, not to be so primly virtuous, after all.

The tantalization of sex is by no means absent from the novels of Gene Stratton Porter. On the contrary the suggestion is omnipresent; it is only the direct statement that is avoided. There is even the threat of rape in *A Girl of the Limberlost*, where Pete Corson watches Elnora in her bedroom with only rotten mosquito netting between them. The readers of Porter's day were titillated by the suggestion of sex, but they shrank—at least her readership shrank—from the bald treatment of it. Porter's heroines are creatures of flesh and blood—real living people. The Angel, Elnora, Mary Malone, Kate Bates, Mahala Spellman, Linda Strong; none of these is modeled on the simpering, swooning, depending heroine of post-Victorian romance. And they are women of action, they are sexually aggressive (in a genteel manner, of course) and they confront life and make it conform to their wishes and desires.

Porter was more successful in depicting the women in her novels than she was in dealing with her men. Her male characters are more like types than like individuals, and they are of a singleness of character. They are either all good or all bad; there is little or no admixture of those traits which make a man what he is—neither all good nor all bad, but human. The prime example is, of course, David Langston, the Harvester. He epitomizes all that is noble in man, even failing to succumb to normal jealousy when Ruth seems to prefer another.

The epitome of good *is* balanced by the epitome of evil, but the balance is achieved through the introduction of an opposing character, not by the commingling of traits in the same person. The Harvester is opposed by Henry Jameson, Ruth's grasping uncle; Freckles by Black Jack, the timber thief; Jason Peters by Junior Moreland *(The White Flag);* and Donald Whiting by Oka Sayye, the unscrupulous Oriental *(Her Father's Daughter).* There is even an instance in *A Girl of the Limberlost* where by indirection the evil of Pete Corson is contrasted with the good of Wesley Sinton. Pete Corson is also the one Porter male character who does display to a small extent a mingling of traits—he resists the temptation to rape Elnora and warns her of her danger from himself. Sometimes the contrast is between strength and weakness rather than between good and evil. Philip Ammon is paired with dilletante Hart Henderson *(A Girl of the Limberlost),* in much the same way that Elnora herself is opposed by Edith Carr, but these women are both strong, almost ruthless, while the men are passive, acquiescent.

The stuff of melodrama is not often to be found in the writing of Gene Stratton Porter. There is little hysteria. Even in her most sentimental passages, she does not attempt to force emotion; she quietly generates emotion by drawing an accurate picture of life during a tense moment. This is not always the case; for example, the overreaction of Elnora to Philip Ammon's asking for a kiss certainly approaches melodrama, as does the whole incident of Kate's giving birth to Elnora. But rather than melodrama these are the expected reactions of idealized characters in the moralistic world of the women's magazines.

Perhaps Porter failed to achieve the greatness she so desired as a novelist because her imagination was undernourished on inadequate experience. Her horizons were limited; she knew only the locale and the people of an extremely narrow and uncharacteristic area. For the swamplands and the swamp people were different from the farmland and farm people of closely neighboring areas of Northeast Indiana. Perhaps broader horizons and wider acquaintance are necessary for good fiction. But she knew her section of the land in minutest detail. She possessed keen powers of observation which enabled her to know her surroundings and the people of her particular milieu. Perhaps this keen observation and this faithful reproduction of a small segment of America could justify Gene Stratton Porter a place in the history of American letters as a local colorist.

It is only by definition that Gene Stratton Porter is not a local color writer.[4] She wrote novels rather than short stories. But the two "Laddie" stories of the *Metropolitan* and other pieces she wrote for magazines and the short pieces in *After the Flood* and *Morning Face* are certainly examples of regionalism. Her handling of dialect was uneven to say the least. When she let her characters speak naturally in the vernacular of the Limberlost as she did in *Freckles,* her reproduction was faithful and not strained, but when she attempted to write Hoosier dialect in the manner of James Whitcomb Riley, she was to put it charitably unsucessful. Nevertheless, her Indiana novels reproduce the differences between the world of which she wrote and that other world with compelling accuracy. She was a spokesman for an otherwise inarticulate portion of the population—she recreated a way of life, and it was a way of life closely akin to that which millions of people caught in the web of urbanization had only recently lost, and to which they longed to return, at least in the pages of romantic fiction.

Perhaps the stigma of having clothed nature in fiction kept Gene Stratton Porter from being recognized as the great nature authority she was. It is a rare reader indeed who displays an equal interest in sentimental romance and serious natural history. And while the vast numbers of Porter's reading public were not deterred by the background of woods and fields and swamps in which her characters acted out their little dramas, scientists were unwilling to sift out the nature from the fiction, no matter how accurate the observations of the former might be. It was only after the results of the reading of her faithful followers began to be revealed in an ever increasing interest in nature and the out of doors, and when nature study—not of course solely, but not negligibly either, due to the influence of Gene Stratton Porter—came to be an integral part of the curriculum in the public schools, that the natural historians began to take a closer look at the nature books of Porter.

Although today's ornithologists can point to errors in Gene Stratton Porter's knowledge of bird life, she combined artistry with skillful observation and somewhat proudly claimed that she was the first to present birds in a completely natural setting. Of course, Audubon and many others had attempted the same thing with some degree of success, but Porter wrote about the birds in the same manner as she depicted them. Her lifelong familiarity with birds and her keen observation of them enabled her to write of their habits and behaviors with the same perception she utilized in her photographing of them. The two went hand in hand. She was never a scientific naturalist; she was a nature lover. For her own taste and to bolster the perfect authenticity of her nature writing, she did study the scientific nature works relating to her own interests. But she was not interested in botany, entomology, or especially ornithology as fields of study. She wanted them as proof. She knew her accounts were true, that she was reporting what she actually had seen, but she wanted the verification of science—this is the attitude that is reflected in her writing.

Critics of writing concerning nature, perhaps influenced by the adverse criticism of the novels by litterateurs, passed over the writings of Porter in favor of those of John Burroughs, Enos Mills, John Muir, and Luther Burbank. Joseph Wood Krutch, anthologizing the "great" nature writing of America in 1950, failed to include Porter. John Kieran, who put out a collection not so selective as Krutch's and containing sixty pieces both by unknowns and by people like Roosevelt, Burroughs, and Peattie, also ignored Porter. And yet, a comparison of almost any passage from *Homing with the Birds* or *Tales You Won't Believe* with any of the writings selected by Krutch or Kieran discloses an equal or even superior accuracy of reporting plus a readability not often found in the writing of the naturalists included by these editors.[5]

It is true that the flourishing sentimentality which characterizes much of Porter's fiction does creep into her nature writing. It is true that at times the human/bird metaphor almost overpowers. But it is also true that there is as much of close and accurate observation and interpretation of nature as there is in almost any of the writing of Burroughs, Muir, or Seton.

Porter liked to compare herself with Fabre and to speculate tht she might have attained a higher plane of recognition had she written in Europe instead of in America. Christopher Morley in the letter quoted also discerned a resemblance to Fabre: "I cannot see that Mrs. Porter's great work with birds is any inferior to the studies of the famous Fabre with insects." In referring to this letter Porter wrote:

You will notice what Mr. Morley says of Fabre. The Fabre books are a part of my religion, but I cannot see that Fabre goes deeper, paints life history more accurately in the case of any insect he has studied than I do in *Moths of the Limberlost*, while my book has the added proof and attraction of the illustration. Yet France went wild over Fabre. I have a feeling very strongly entrenched that if I had made the mark I have on the homes of the United States or written and illustrated my seven nature books in any country in Europe, my reception would be very different for my nature work.[6]

Had Morley read further into the works of Porter, he might have discovered that her knowledge of insects was almost if not quite equal to her knowledge of birds. There was of course *Moths of the Limberlost* but there was also the in-depth acquaintance and fascinating presentation of the life history of bees in *The Keeper of the Bees.*

In attempting an evaluation of the nature writing of Gene Stratton Porter certain findings seem pertinent. Her observations were true, and her pictures—both photographic and word—are authentic. Perhaps she did attempt to humanize the birds a little too much, and perhaps she did apply the same sentimental approach of the novels a little too often, but the fact is that she was able to write interestingly of nature with scientific accuracy although not in scientific jargon. What she wrote, the average American layman could read and understand. But even more importantly, and much more in accord with her intent, readers might be led from the perusal of any of her books directly into the great outdoors itself to see, to appreciate, and to learn to love nature firsthand.

II   *A Conclusion*

Most of Gene Stratton Porter's novels are now nearly forgotten, but interest in the nature books continues and, in fact, seems to be increasing. It can be maintained that she fell victim to changing times; the taste of the reading public altered greatly in the period of the Great Depression, when the affection for the old romantic quest was fading, to be replaced by an allegiance to the realism, naturalism, and satire which were to dominate the 1930s. Porter's death at the height of a rewarding and highly profitable career may have saved her the pain and disappointment of having to watch that career dwindle and fade.

Porter somehow failed to develop major powers of fiction, but then it must be remembered that she never intended her work to be judged solely as fiction but as *story* carrying a nature message. It was her undeniably fine portrayal of a region and her excellent discernment of the wonders of nature which sustained her through many successful years. If she neither knew nor cared how to construct a novel, she certainly possessed the power to weave a narrative and to tell a story. Considered as novels, the books had obvious faults which made literary critics scorn them. The plots were somewhat puerile, the characters had a tendency either to gush or to preach, and frequently the sentiment was too exuberant. But obviating these flaws—for most of her readers— were the facts that the people of whom she wrote were usually simple, honest, and good natured; that through their eyes one saw, and through their actions one experienced, the author's knowledge and love of outdoor things; and that, above all, here was a woman endowed with the real ability to tell a story.

As the years go by in the continuing reappraisal which is the history of American letters, what does the future hold for Gene Stratton Porter? For many years she has been relegated to the ranks of popular but inconsequential writers. This neglect is unjust in view of her actual range and versatility. In the reaction against the overromantic and sentimental novels and novelists of the early part of the century; the authors most properly attuned to their own and to past time were thrust farthest from the public gaze. In this sense, Porter belongs to a misunderstood past, a past which critics and historians of the last quarter of this century are willing to re-examine and to re-evaluate. It seems certain that no critic hereafter can refer to the popular culture of Porter's time and not feel the importance of her contribution to it. As the years go by it seems quite probable that Gene Stratton Porter will be elevated to a secure place among the minor American authors.

Notes and References

Chapter One

1. *The Women Who Make Our Novels* (Freeport, N.Y., 1967), p. 313. This book is a reprint of the 1928 edition. Overton wrote three books in which Porter is considered. For complete information see Selected Bibliography, Secondary Sources.

2. "An American Bird Woman," *Chambers Journal* [London] XLVI (Sept. and Oct. 1914), 538ff, 636ff.

3. Porter, "My Life and My Books," *Ladies' Home Journal* XXIII (Sept. 1916), 13, 80–81.

4. *Gene Stratton-Porter: A Little Story of the Life and Work and Ideals of "The Bird Woman"* (Garden City, N.Y., 1926), pp. 2–52; reprint issued from the 1915 edition by Doubleday after Porter's death.

5. "Gene Stratton-Porter," *The Country Life Press* (Garden City, N.Y., 1919), pp. 141–48; a series of sketches of the leading authors in the Doubleday stable.

6. Grace D. Rose, "Limberlost Lady: A Story of Gene Stratton–Porter," TS. in Indiana State Library, Indianapolis, n.d., p.18.

7. J. F. Snow, *Snow's History of Adams County, Indiana* (Indianapolis, 1907), p. 464.

8. Flossie Enyart Bailey, *Pioneer Days in the Wabash Valley* (Logansport, Indiana, 1933), p. 80.

9. *The Lady of the Limberlost: The Life and Letters of Gene Stratton-Porter* (Garden City, N.Y., 1928), p. 228; further references to this volume are cited as "Meehan."

10. Porter, "The Gift of the Birds," *Youth's Companion* LXXXVIII (Mar. 19 and Mar. 26, 1914), pp. 147–48, 159–60; also in *Homing with the Birds* (Garden City, N.Y., 1919), pp. 21–33.

11. Porter, "What My Father Meant to Me," *American Magazine* XCIX (Feb. 1925), 23, 70, 72, 76.

12. Meehan, p. 314; letter to Porter from William Sloan Kennedy.

13. Meehan, p. 131; letter from Porter to a San Francisco reviewer.

14. Porter, "The Influence of Clothes," *Let Us Highly Resolve* (Garden City, N.Y., 1927), p. 286.

15. Meehan, p. 49; letter from Geneve Stratton to Mr. Porter.

16. Herbert R. Hill, "Limberlost Author: Gene Stratton Porter," *Outdoor Indiana* XXXIII (Apr. 1968), 26.

17. Meehan, p. 83.

18. Ibid., p. 88.

19. "Life and Writings," *Bookman* XLI (1915), 593-94.

20. Meehan, p. 112; from an unidentified writing of Porter's.

21. Ibid., pp. 226, 230-31; from a letter written by Porter to an unidentified recipient.

22. "Gene Stratton-Porter, Best Seller" (Fort Wayne, Indiana, 1953), n.p., but 5 by count.

23. Meehan, p. 99.

24. Mrs. Frank N. Wallace (Lorene Miller), "Gene Stratton-Porter Started Famous Story 'The Harvester' on Valentine's Day 28 Years Ago," *Indianapolis Sunday Star Magazine*, Feb. 12, 1939, p. 28.

25. Meehan, pp. 99-110; paper written by Porter entitled, "My Estimate of Walt Whitman," and unpublished elsewhere.

26. Meehan, p. 126.

27. Ibid., pp. 194-95.

28. Ibid., p. 123; unidentified writing of Porter, retold in numerous other sources.

29. Saxton, pp. 26-27; a much fuller account of the preparation of this second story than is given in Meehan (pp. 125-26).

30. Meehan, pp. 126-27; Meehan's account plus a description of Porter in a letter from her sister, Florence Compton.

31. "Gene Stratton-Porter's Page: A Message to the Working Woman," *McCall's* XXIII (July 1926), 2.

32. Mrs. Wallace, "Extended Search for Renowned Fringed Gentian with Late Gene Stratton-Porter Is Described," *Indianapolis Sunday Star Magazine*, Oct. 18, 1936, p. 4.

33. Porter, "The Search for Three Birds," *Tales You Won't Believe* (Garden City, N.Y., 1925), pp. 172-73.

34. Ibid., p. 175.

35. Meehan, p. 197; letter from Porter to friends in Scotland.

36. Ibid., p. 273, italics supplied; letter from Porter to Mrs. Adeline Higbee.

37. Jeannette Porter Meehan, "My Mother," *McCall's* LII (June 1925), 18-19, 76.

Chapter Two

1. Meehan, p. 302; a writing of Porter's replying to her critics, seemingly put together from the *Bookman* [London] and *Ladies' Home Journal* articles.

2. Review of *Michael O'Halloran*, *Athenaeum* [London] II (1918), 190.

3. Tasker W. Witham, *The Adolescent in the American Novel* (New York, 1964), pp. 9-10.

4. Hazel Sample, *Pitfalls for Readers of Fiction*: Pamphlet Publication of the National Council of Teachers of English, No. 1 (Chicago, 1939–40), pp. 1–35; illustrates "pitfalls" by comparing assumptions in the writings of Zane Grey, Harold Bell Wright, Gene Stratton Porter, and Emilie Loring.

5. Jane S. Bakerman, "Gene Stratton-Porter Reconsidered," *Kate Chopin Newsletter* II: 3 (Winter 1976–77), 3–4.

6. Meehan, pp. 267–72; letter written by Porter to her sister, Florence Compton.

7. Porter, *The Keeper of the Bees* (New York, 1925), pp. 83–87.

8. Porter, *The Harvester* (New York, 1911), pp. 302–305.

9. Frank N. Wallace, *Gene Stratton-Porter and Her Studies of Native Plants*, paper read at March meeting of Garden Flowers Society of Fort Wayne, 1925, TS., p. 3, in Indiana State Library, Indianapolis.

10. Porter, "My Ideal Home," *Country Life in America* XL (Oct. 1921), 40–43.

11. "Search for Three Birds," pp. 155–80.

12. Review of *Friends in Feathers, Independent* XIX (July 21, 1917), 110.

13. Meehan, pp. 305–306; Porter writing a response to her critics.

14. Porter, "Bird Architecture," *Outing* XXXVIII (1901), 437–42.

15. "My Work and My Critics," *Bookman* [London] XLIX (1916), 149.

16. "Mrs. Porter and Nature," *Bookman* XXXV (1912), 588.

17. Meehan, p. 134.

18. Saxton, pp. 26–27.

19. Porter, "What My Father Meant to Me,", 23ff.

20. Porter, "Why I always Wear My Rose Colored Glasses," *American Magazine* LXXXVIII (Aug. 1919), 36–37, 112, 114–15, 118, 121.

21. Ibid., p. 114.

22. Meehan, pp. 224–25.

23. Porter, "My Ideal Home," *Country Life in America* XL (Oct. 1921), 40–43; this article is one of a ten-part series dealing with the ideal homes of famous people—this issue discusses homes of Robert Louis Stevenson, David Belasco, Josef Hoffman, and Porter.

24. Porter, "The Making of a Great Ranch", *Country Life* XI (Jan. 1907), 298–302.

25. Phelps, "Why of Best Sellers," *Bookman* LIV (Dec. 1921), 300.

26. Meehan, p. 234, see also p. 257.

27. Porter, "Blue Eyed Mary," *Good Housekeeping* LXXII (May 1921), 52.

28. Meehan, p. 227; letter written by Porter to unknown recipient.

29. Porter, *The Firebird* (Garden City, N.Y., 1922), pp. 17–18.

30. Meehan, pp. 232–34; letter written by Porter to her friend, Mrs. J. W. McCamish of Winchester, Indiana.

31. Meehan, p. 246; unidentified quotation from Porter, but see *McCall's* editorial of July 1922.

32. Meehan, p. 250; letter from Porter to Mrs. Anne Pennebaker.

33. Porter, "Euphorbia," *Good Housekeeping* LXXVI (Jan. 1923), 12.

34. Meehan, p. 232; letter to Mrs. McCamish.

35. Porter, *Jesus of the Emerald*, 1st ed. (Garden City, N.Y., 1923), n.p., but 8-9 by count.

36. Porter,"Whitmore's Bull," *McCall's* LIII (June 1926), 9, 48.

37. Meehan, p. 247; letter from Porter to Dr. Charles Wharton Stork.

38. Ibid., p. 230; from same unidentified letter as n. 28, above.

39. Ibid. p. 251; letter to Mrs. Pennebaker.

40. Ibid., p. 247-48; letter to Dr. Stork.

41. Porter, *Homing with the Birds* (Garden City, N.Y., 1919), pp. 51, 53.

42. *Artists in Indiana—Then and Now: Gene Stratton-Porter, Photographer*, Exhibition Pamphlet, Art Gallery, Ball State University, William E. Story, Dir. (Muncie, Indiana, 1976), n.p.

43. *Homing*, p. 61.

44. Ibid., p. 64.

45. An advertisement at Limberlost Cabin (Geneva) indicates that this film was *Freckles*, produced by Paramount Pictures and starring Jack Pickford.

46. Meehan, p. 240.

47. *Gene Stratton Porter State Memorial*. Pamphlet, Division of Museums & Memorials, Indiana Department of Natural Resources (Indianapolis, n.d.), n.p.

48. David G. MacLean, "Movie Ephemera," *Gene Stratton-Porter: A Bibliography and Collector's Guide* (Decatur, Indiana, 1976), p. 105; hereafter referred to as "MacLean."

49. Meehan, pp. 245-46; unidentified quotation from Porter's writing.

50. MacLean, p. 116.

51. Mr. Rollin King, Muncie, Indiana, provided numerous news clippings identifying Miss Minahan.

52. *Bookman* [London], p. 152.

53. Porter, "From the Viewpoint of a Field Worker," *The American Annual of Photography and Photographic Times Almanac for 1902*, Walter E. Woodbury, ed. (New York, 1901), pp. 214-226.

Chapter Three

1. Saxton, p. 37.

2. Review of *Freckles, New York Times, Saturday Review of Books*, Dec. 3, 1904, p. 839.

3. Porter, "My Work and My Critics," *Bookman* [London], 149.

4. MacLean, p. 2; from the Publisher's Synopsis of *At the Foot of the Rainbow*.

5. Meehan, p. 138; but in many places a "contract" with her publishers is spoken of.

6. Review of *The Harvester, New York Times, Saturday Review of Books*, Sept. 17, 1911, p. 554.

7. Meehan, p. 170; letter written by Porter in answer to a letter of inquiry from a reader.

8. Meehan, p. 178; an unidentified writing by Porter.

9. , "How Laddie and the Princess Spelled Down at the Christmas Bee," *Metropolitan* XIV (Dec. 1901), 753; this passage does not appear in the novel *Laddie*.

10. Meehan, p. 18.

11. Porter, "My Life and My Books," *Ladies' Home Journal*, p. 80.

12. Porter, *Michael O'Halloran*, p. 77.

13. MacLean, p. 9; Publisher's Synopsis of *A Daughter of the Land*.

14. Review of *A Daughter of the Land, Publisher's Weekly* XCIV (Aug. 17, 1918), 555.

15. Hill, " 'Limberlost' Author,'', p. 27.

16. Porter, *Her Father's Daughter*, p. 76.

17. Meehan, p. 254.

18. MacLean, pp. 68–69; Publisher's Synopsis of *The White Flag*.

19. Porter, *The Keeper of the Bees*, pp. 196–212.

20. Hill, " 'Limberlost' Author," p. 38.

21. Meehan, p. 297.

22. Correspondence with Anastasia Hathaway referring to a letter, unfortunately undated, from Jeannette Porter Meehan, describing the visit Porter and Meehan made to President Roosevelt.

Chapter Four

1. For a few examples of the charge of pride leveled against Porter see *Bookman* XXV (Aug. 1907), 622; *Dial* XLIII (Oct. 1, 1907), 216; *Review* I (Nov. 15, 1919), 586; *London Times Literary Supplement*, Nov. 27, 1919, p. 687.

2. Meehan, pp. 210–11; letter from Christopher Morley to Mr. F. N. Doubleday.

3. Porter, *Homing with the Birds*, p. 9.

4. Ibid., p. 337.

5. Ibid., pp. 121–22.

6. Herbert K. Job, "The Wood Duck," in *Birds of America*, ed. T. Gilbert Pearson (Garden City, N.Y., 1936), p. 129.

7. Porter, *Homing*, pp. 122–23.

8. Ibid., p. 374.

9. Meehan, pp. 138–39; unidentified writing by Porter.

10. Porter, *Tales You Won't Believe*, p. 65.

11. Meehan, p. 261; letter to Mrs. Pennebaker.

12. Ibid., p. 211; unfortunately, Meehan fails further to identify Dr. Emerson.

13. Mrs. Wallace, "Snow Bound at Limberlost Cabin," *Indianapolis Sunday Star Magazine*, Feb. 25, 1940, p. 4; *Bookman* [London], p. 154.

14. Meehan, pp. 190-91.

15. "Indiana Author's Book to be Staged: Geneva Woman Called to Europe to Assist in the Work of Preparation," *Muncie Star Book Section*, Nov. 11, 1905, p. 1; Mr. Rollin King of Muncie supplied this information and the clipping.

16. *Gene Stratton Porter State Memorial*, Pamphlet.

17. *Indiana: A Guide to the Hoosier State* (New York, 1941), p. 424.

18. Mrs. Wallace, "Famous Story, 'The Harvester,'" p. 3.

19. Review of *Song of the Cardinal*, *Arena* XXX (Aug. 1903), 215.

20. Meehan, p. 169, unidentified writing by Porter.

21. *Bookman* [London], p. 151.

22. "Moths of the Limberlost," *Book Review Digest* (1912), p. 336; but quotes Publisher's Synopsis as in MacLean, p. 56.

23. *Moths of the Limberlost*, pp. 130-33; *A Girl of the Limberlost* (Gossett and Dunlap edition), pp. 244-46; *Tales You Won't Believe*, pp. 11-15.

24. Porter, "Hidden Treasures," *Country Life* XXII (June 15, 1912), 36.

25. Porter, *Music of the Wild*, p. 35.

26. Ibid., p. 198.

27. Ibid., pp. 218, 222.

28. Ibid., pp. 289, 301, 302.

29. Ibid., p. 331.

30. Ibid., pp. 332, 335.

31. Porter, *Tales You Won't Believe*, pp. 129-30.

32. Porter, "The Dog That Will Never Be Kicked Again," *Literary Digest* LXXXI (May 24, 1924), 59-63.

33. Porter, *Tales You Won't Believe*, p. 112.

34. Ibid., p. 230.

35. Ibid., pp. 172-73.

36. Ibid., p. 175.

Chapter Five

1. Porter, *Let Us Highly Resolve*, p. 335.

2. Joseph Newman, ed., *200 Years: A Bicentennial Illustrated History of the United States* (Washington, D.C., 1973), II, 89; all further statistics unless specifically noted are taken from this volume.

3. Accounts of emigrants stopping at the Strattons are to be found in "Am I My Brother's Keeper" in *Let Us Highly Resolve* (p. 63), and in the novel *Laddie* (passim).

4. Hathaway letter; unfortunately, date not given.

5. Porter, "Are Women Fair in Politics?" *McCall's* L (Dec. 1922), 2, 33.

6. Meehan, see especially pp. 95-96, 127, 235, 264.

7. Ibid., see especially pp. 194-97, 200, 213.

8. Saxton, p. 44; but on page 46 he changes the figure to 1,666; the World Trade Center is 1,350 feet tall; the Sears Tower, 1,454 feet.

9. Alice Payne Hackett, *70 Years of Best Sellers, 1895-1965* (New York, 1967), p. 7; unidentified references to best-sellerism are to this volume.

10. Suzanne Ellery Greene, *Books for Pleasure* (Bowling Green, Ohio, 1947) p. 162; this definition also occurs in Mott's book (No. 13, below), also in 1947.

11. The lists of best-sellers used in the preparation of this book are those from *Publishers' Weekly* as reported in Hackett.

12. Meehan, p. 255.

13. Frank Luther Mott, *Golden Multitudes: The Story of Best Sellers in the United States* (New York, 1947, 3d printing, 1966), p. 218.

14. John William Tebbel, *A History of Book Publishing in the United States*, Vol. II, *The Expansion of an Industry* (New York, 1975), p. 653.

15. MacLean, p. 113; however, the present research for this book has discovered almost a hundred more, not in MacLean.

16. Tebbel, p. 170.

17. Bernard Berelson, "Who Reads What Books and Why?" *Saturday Review of Literature*, May 12, 1951, p. 7.

18. Irving Harlow Hart, "The One Hundred Leading Authors of Best Sellers in Fiction from 1895 to 1944," *Publishers' Weekly* CXLIX: 3 (Jan. 19, 1946), 285; see also in *PW*, "The Most Popular Authors of Fiction between 1900 and 1925" (Feb. 21, 1925), and "The Most Popular Authors of Fiction in the Post-war Period, 1919 to 1926" (Mar. 12, 1927).

19. Tebbel, p. 79.

20. Ibid., p. 331.

21. Porter, "Why I Always Wear My Rose Colored Glasses," p. 118.

22. R. Baird Shuman, *William Inge* [TUSAS 95] (New York, 1965), p. 173.

23. Review, *Song of the Cardinal*, *Arena*, p. 215.

24. Frederic Taber Cooper, "The Popularity of Gene Stratton-Porter," *Bookman* XLI (Aug. 1915), 670.

25. Ibid.

26. Review of *Keeper of the Bees*, *New York Times Book Section*, Aug. 16, 1925, p. 7.

27. Review of *Keeper of the Bees, New York World Book Section*, Aug. 16, 1925, p. 3.

28. Van Doren, *The American Novel: 1789-1939* (New York, 1940), p. 269.

29. Overton, *American Nights Entertainment* (New York, 1923), pp. 286, 272-73.

30. Russell Nye, *The Unembarrassed Muse: The Popular Arts in America* (New York, 1970), p. 38.

31. LHUS, p. 1121.

32. *Bookman* [London], pp. 151-52.

33. Cooper, p. 670.

34. Meehan, p. 258.

35. Phelps, p. 301.

36. Ibid.

37. Review of *Tales You Won't Believe, New York Tribune Book Section*, May 17, 1925, p. 3.

Chapter Six

1. Meehan, p. 159.

2. Bakerman, p. 3.

3. Brooks, *Sketches in Criticism* (New York, 1932), pp. 226-27.

4. Claude M. Simpson, ed., *The Local Colorists: American Short Story, 1857-1900* (New York, 1960), pp. 2-3; limits local color to short fiction rather than to novels.

5. Krutch, *Great American Nature Writing* (New York, 1950); Kieran, *John Kieran's Treasury of Great Nature Writing* (Garden City, N.Y., 1957).

6. Meehan, p. 210; the Morley letter is found on pp. 210-11.

Selected Bibliography

PRIMARY SOURCES

1. Fiction

Books are arranged chronologically by date of publication. There have been almost three hundred different editions or reprintings of the novels; in this list only the first publication for each title is given. If a different edition has been used in preparation of the text, that edition is documented in the Notes and References section.

The Song of the Cardinal. Indianapolis: Bobbs-Merrill, 1903.
Freckles. New York: Doubleday, Page & Company, 1904.
At the Foot of the Rainbow. New York: The Outing Publishing Company, 1907.
A Girl of the Limberlost. New York: Doubleday, Page & Company, 1909.
The Harvester. Garden City, N.Y.: Doubleday, Page & Company, 1911.
Laddie. Garden City, N.Y.: Doubleday, Page & Company, 1913.
Michael O'Halloran. Garden City, N.Y.: Doubleday, Page & Company, 1915.
A Daughter of the Land. Garden City, N.Y.: Doubleday, Page & Company, 1918.
Her Father's Daughter. Garden City, N.Y., and Toronto: Doubleday, Page & Company, 1921.
The White Flag. Garden City, N.Y.: Doubleday, Page & Company, 1923. [Serialization in Good Housekeeping, April through November 1923.]
The Keeper of the Bees. Garden City, N.Y.: Doubleday, Page & Company, 1921. "Gene Stratton-Porter: Her Life and Her Books" appended, pp. 507–15. [Serialization in McCall's February through September 1925.]
The Magic Garden. Garden City, N.Y.: Doubleday, Page & Company, 1927. [Serialization in McCall's October 1926 through March 1927.]

2. Nature Books

What I Have Done with Birds: Character Studies of Native American Birds which through Friendly Advance I Induced to Pose for Me, or

Succeeded in Photographing by Good Fortune, with the Story of My Experiences in Obtaining Their Pictures. Indianapolis; Bobbs-Merrill, 1907.

Birds of the Bible. Cincinnati: Jennings & Graham/New York: Eaton & Mains, 1909.

Music of the Wild: With Reproductions of the Performers, Their Instruments and Festival Halls. Cincinnati: Jennings & Graham/New York: Eaton & Mains, 1910.

Moths of the Limberlost. Garden City, N.Y.: Doubleday, Page & Company, 1912.

Friends in Feathers. [Revised and enlarged edition of *What I Have Done with Birds.*] Garden City, N.Y.: Doubleday, Page & Company, 1917.

Homing with the Birds: The History of a Lifetime of Personal Experience with the Birds. Garden City, N.Y.: Doubleday, Page & Company, 1919.

Wings. Garden City, N.Y.: Doubleday, Page & Company, 1923. [Selected and edited chapters from previous books.]

Tales You Won't Believe. Garden City, N.Y:: Doubleday, Page & Company, 1925.

3. Poetry

Although never published in book form, the poem *Euphorbia,* because of its length and importance, is included with the books of poetry.

The Firebird. Garden City, N.Y., and Toronto: Doubleday, Page & Company, 1922.

Euphorbia. Good Housekeeping, LXXVI, January through March 1923.

Jesus of the Emerald. Garden City, N.Y.: Doubleday, Page & Company, 1923.

4. Miscellany

After the Flood. Indiana Society of Chicago, *The Hoosier Set,* vol. 8. Indianapolis: Bobbs-Merrill Co., 1911. [Children's book.]

Birds of the Limberlost: Especially prepared for Miss Katharine Minahan. Garden City, N.Y.: Doubleday, Page & Company, 1914. [Programme.]

Morning Face. Garden City, N.Y.: Doubleday, Page & Company, 1916. [Children's book.]

Let Us Highly Resolve. Garden City, N.Y.: Doubleday, Page & Company, 1927. [Collection of essays—mostly reprinted from *McCall's.*]

5. Publications in Periodicals

Almost two hundred publications in magazines and newspapers by Gene Stratton Porter have been located. Only works of special interest or pertinence to this study are listed here. For a more inclusive number see David MacLean's *Bibliography* (below). Items here given are arranged alphabetically by magazine and chronologically by appearance. Works reprinted in books are not listed as separate items, but the serialization is indicated.

American Magazine.
"Why I Always Wear My Rose Colored Glasses," LXXXVIII (August 1919), 36–37, 112, 114–15, 118, 121.
"What My Father Meant to Me," XCIX (February 1925), 23, 70, 72, 76.
Bookman [London].
"My Work and My Critics," XLIX (February 1916), 147–55.
Country Life in America.
"The Making of a Great Ranch," XI (January 1907), 298–302.
"Hidden Treasures: Moths of the Limberlost," XXII (June 1912), 29–36.
"My Ideal Home," XL (October 1921), 40–43.
Good Housekeeping.
"Blue Eyed Mary" [Poem], LXXII (May 1921), 52.
"Euphorbia" [Poem], LXXVI (January 1923), 10–13; (February 1923), 24–26; (March 1923), 42–45.
"The White Flag" [Serialization of novel], LXXVI–LXXVII (April through November 1923).
"Tales You Won't Believe" [Serialization of nature book], LXXVIII–LXXX (January 1924 through February 1925).
"Let Us Go Back to Poetry," LXXX (April 1925), 34–35, 194–96, 199–200.
Ladies' Home Journal.
"What I Have Done with Birds" [Serialization of nature book], XXIII (April through August 1906).
"My Life and My Books," XXXIII (September 1916), 13, 80–81.
Literary Digest.
"The Dog That Will Never Be Kicked Again," LXXXI (May 24, 1924), 59–63.
McCall's Magazine.
[From December 1921 through December 1927, Porter appeared in every issue of McCall's. Much of the series, "Gene Stratton-Porter's Page," was reprinted in *Let Us Highly Resolve.* Only significant omissions are included here. The MacLean book is

particularly weak in this instance, some fifty items being omitted.]
"Gene Stratton-Porter Calls on Our Government to Curb Indecent Literature," LXIX (July 1922), 1, 18.
"Our Churches, Our Schools, and Our Colleges," L (October 1922), 2, 64.
"A New Day in Pictures," L (February 1923), 2, 47, 89.
"Modern Methods of Teaching School," L (June 1923), 2, 55, 57, 80.
"The Keeper of the Bees" [Serialization of novel], LII-LIII (February through August 1925).
"The Bible in the Schools," LII (May 1925), 2, 78.
"Shall Girls Pay Their Way?" LII (August 1925), 2, 48.
"Whitmore's Bull" [Poem], LIII (June 1926), 8-9, 84, 102-103.
"The Magic Garden" [Serialization of novel], LIV (October 1926 through March 1927).
"Advice for Aspiring Poets," LIV (March 1927), 142.
"The Disadvantages of Authorship," LIV (May 1927), 136.
"Personal Adventures as an Author," LIV (June 1927), 2.
Metropolitan Magazine.
"Laddie, the Princess, and the Pie," XIV (September 1901), 416, 421.
"How Laddie and the Princess Spelled Down at the Christmas Bee," XIV (December 1901), 739-53.
"When Luck Is Golden," XV (April 1902), 440-45.
"The Real Babes in the Woods," XVI (August 1902), 201-13.
"Bob's Feathered Interloper," XVII (November 1903), 192-203.
Outdoor America.
"My Great Day," II (June 1924), 12-14.
Outing.
"Bird Architecture," XXXVIII (July 1901), 437-42.
"Photographing the Belted Kingfisher," XXXIX (November 1901), 198-202.
"A Study of the Black Vulture," XXXIX (December 1901), 279-83.
"The Birds' Kindergarten," XL (April 1902), 70-74.
"Sight and Scent in Animals and Birds," XL (June 1902), 295-98.
"The Music of the Marsh," XL (September 1902), 658-65.
Recreation.
[All publication in *Recreation* was by-lined "Gene S. Porter."]
"A New Experience in Millinery," XII (February 1900), 115.
"Why the Biggest One Got Away," XII (April 1900), 265-68.
"In the Camps of Croesus," XIII (July 1900), 21-22.
"Camera Notes" [By-lined column], (January, April, July 1900; January, February, March, May 1901).
World's Work.
"Why I Wrote 'A Girl of the Limberlost,'" XIX (February 1910), 12545-47.
Youth's Companion.

"The Gift of the Birds," LXXXVIII (March 19, 1914), 147–48; (March 26, 1914), 159–60.

SECONDARY SOURCES

1. Bibliography

MacLean, David G. *Gene Stratton-Porter: A Bibliography and Collector's Guide*. Decatur, Indiana: Americana Books, 1976. A comprehensive listing of Porter's output as an author, it would have saved this writer much investigation had it been published before the present research was almost completed. However, this researcher discovered many items not in MacLean which are identified in the Notes and References, Primary Sources, or in this section. The material on the collectibility of Porter's books indicates that modern interest in this writer is increasing.

2. Biography

Maule, H. E. "Gene Stratton-Porter: A Little Story of the Life and Work and Ideals of 'The Bird Woman.'" In *Doubleday, Page and Company*. [Published for the friends of Doubleday, Page & Company.] Garden City, N.Y.: The Country Life Press, 1919. A reissue of the Saxton booklet listed below with slight alterations. Also appended to 1925 edition of *The Keeper of the Bees* (pp. 507–15) with minor updating under the title "Gene Stratton-Porter: Her Life and Her Books."

Meehan, Jeannette Porter. *The Lady of the Limberlost: The Life and Letters of Gene Stratton-Porter*. Garden City, N.Y.: Doubleday, Doran & Company, Inc., 1928. The subjective biography of Porter written by her daughter but compiled from other sources—Saxton, Maule, and various magazine articles—as well as from family history, personal reminiscence, and the author's correspondence. Useful but confusing because of lack of or conflict among dates and failure to name the recipients or senders of many of the letters. To be read for pleasure rather than scholarly pursuit, but still the main source for information about Porter.

S. F. E., compiler. *Gene Stratton-Porter: A Little Story of Her Life and Work*. Garden City, N.Y.: Doubleday, Page & Company, 1915. Reprinted 1926. This volume identified only by the initials, S. F. E. is generally attributed to Eugene Francis Saxton in spite of the unusual reversal of the initials. Copies in the Indiana State Library and in Indiana University Library attribute the book to Sam F. Ewart. The 1926 printing has two title pages, the first bearing the subtitle given above at Maule, the second as given here. The

copyright is given as by Porter in 1915 and by Doubleday in 1926.
At any rate, this booklet is probably the biographical sketch of
Porter's life that she wished her readers to have.

3. Books

BAILEY, FLOSSIE ENYART. *Pioneer Days in the Wabash Valley: With a
Review of the Life of Gene Stratton-Porter.* Logansport, Indiana:
Hendricks Bros., 1933. Valuable background material, especially
concerning the Stratton family and the years spent in Wabash,
Indiana.

BANTA, R[ICHARD] E[WELL], ed. *Hoosier Caravan: A Treasury of Indiana
Life and Lore,* new and enlarged edition. Bloomington, Indiana:
Indiana University Press, 1975. The standard history of Indiana
letters; the material on Porter was taken mainly from *Who's Who
in America.*

GREENE, SUZANNE ELLERY. *Books for Pleasure: Popular Fiction,
1914-1945.* Bowling Green, Ohio: Bowling Green University
Popular Press, 1947. A scholarly book about popular culture. Does
not denigrate, but views dispassionately the writers and the times
in which they wrote; has many references to Porter.

HACKETT, ALICE PAYNE. *70 Years of Best Sellers, 1895-1965.* New York: R.
R. Bowker Company, 1967. Extremely useful source of information
on the sales of Porter's novels and her comparative position among
other writers of the day. Based on the records of *Publishers'
Weekly,* of which Ms. Hackett was (1967) a staff member. Follows
two other volumes dealing with forty and fifty years of best-
sellerdom.

HART, JAMES DAVID. *The Popular Book, A History of America's Literary
Taste.* Berkeley and Los Angeles: University of California Press,
1963. An account of the times and the culture including the years
in which Porter lived, it deals with the forces that shaped the
tastes of the reading public in that era.

HOCKEY, DOROTHY. "The Good and the Beautiful: A Study of Best Selling
Novels in America, 1895-1920." Diss. Western Reserve, 1947.
Covers only the early part of Porter's career.

HOEKSTRA, ELLEN. "The Pedestal Myth Reinforced: Women's Magazine
Fiction, 1900-1920." In *New Dimensions in Popular Culture,* ed.
Russel B. Nye. Bowling Green, Ohio: Bowling Green University
Popular Press, 1972, pp. 43-58. A sprightly discussion of the
influence of the women's magazines on fiction writers (including
Porter) of the first twenty years of the century. Deals with the
emphasis on sincerity, constancy, and virtue.

INDIANA: A Guide to the Hoosier State. Compiled by Workers of the
Writers' Program of the Works Progress Administration in the

State of Indiana. [American Guide Series.] New York: Oxford University Press, second printing with corrections, 1945. Gives an overview of the state and especially of the region which produced Porter, its geology, geography, and history; has a section dealing with Indiana authors.

LEHMAN HAUPT, HELMUT (in collaboration with LAWRENCE C. WORTH and ROLLO G. SILVER). *The Book in America: A History of the Making and Selling of Books in the United States*, 2d edition. New York: R. R. Bowker Company, 1952. While devoid of specific information about Porter, contains a wealth of information about book publishing in general and about her publishers, Doubleday, Page & Company, in particular.

MOTT, FRANK LUTHER. *Golden Multitudes: The Story of Best Sellers in the United States*. New York and London: R. R. Bowker Co., 1947 (3d printing, 1966). Along with *Hackett* the standard treatise on best-sellers in the Untied States. Contains much information about Porter. See also his *History of American Magazines* published by Harvard University Press.

NYE, RUSSEL. *The Unembarrassed Muse: The Popular Arts in America*. New York: The Dial Press, 1970. An account from the popular-culture point of view which discusses the times of Porter and explains her phenomenal success in writing for those times.

OVERTON, GRANT MARTIN. *American Nights Entertainment*. New York: D. Appleton & Co., 1923. "In the production of this work the author was assisted by four publishing houses: D. Appleton & Co., George H. Doran Company, Doubleday, Page & Co., Charles Scribner's Sons," and the title page bears the names of all four publishers. This work is a reworking of Overton's *Women who Make Our Novels* (1919) and was itself reworked into *Authors of the Day* (1924, reissued 1967). However, the material relating to Porter is best secured through the volume listed above.

PATTEE, FRED LEWIS. *The New American Literature, 1890-1930*. New York: The Century Company, 1930. While bewailing her sentimentality and dismissing her as of little consequence, Pattee is forced to admire her skillful blend of extensive and exact knowledge of nature with fiction.

SHUMAKER, ARTHUR W. *A History of Indiana Literature: With Emphasis on the Authors of Imaginative Works Who Commenced Writing Prior to World War II*. Indianapolis: Indiana Historical Bureau, 1962. [Issued also as Indiana Historical Collections, Vol. XLII.] The published form of Dr. Shumaker's 1958 dissertation of practically the same title at the University of Iowa is, along with *Banta*, a prime source for information about Indiana authors. Gives scholarly interpretation of the writers of the period with numerous references to Porter.

VAN DOREN, CARL. *The American Novel: 1789-1939*. Revised and enlarged edition. New York: The Macmillan Co., 1940. This book, which is a rewriting and reissue of the author's earlier *Contemporary American Novelists: 1900-1920* (1928), contains material almost identical to the first volume when dealing with Porter; he is perhaps her severest critic.

WITHAM, W. TASKER. *The Adolescent in the American Novel*. New York: Frederick Ungar Publishing Company, 1964. A valuable study of Porter's characters as adolescents, and of her books as reading for adolescents.

4. Periodicals

ALLEN, FREDERICK LEWIS. "Best Sellers: 1900-1935. The Trend of Popular Reading since the Turn of the Century." *Saturday Review of Literature*, December 7, 1935, pp. 35-38. Discusses both the forces which made Porter popular and the change in the times which led to the lessening of that appeal.

"An American Bird Woman." *Chambers Journal* [London and Edinburgh], Part 46 (October 1, 1914), 636ff. The English article based on autobiographical information furnished by Porter herself.

"An Appreciation," by C. W. *Bookman* [London] XLIX (February 1916), 145-46. A highly supportive study of Porter emphasizing the fact that her popularity indicated that she possessed some quality that made her appeal to so many readers.

COOPER, FREDERIC TABER. "Popularity of Gene Stratton-Porter." *Bookman* XLI (August 1915), 670-71. Along with a somewhat scathing denunciation of Porter (to which she replied in the London *Bookman*) the article contains much sane evaluation and some stinting praise.

CORDELL, RICHARD A. "Limestone, Corn, and Literature: The Indiana Scene and Its Interpreters." *Saturday Review of Literature*, December 17, 1938, pp. 3-4, 14-15. Attributes at least a part of the popularity of Porter to the fact that she idealized and sentimentalized the Limberlost region of Indiana.

DAHLKE-SCOTT, DEBORAH, and PREWITT, MICHAEL. "A Writer's Crusade to Portray the Spirit of the Limberlost." *Smithsonian* VII: 1 (April 1976), 64-68. A present-day recognition of the talents of Gene Stratton Porter as naturalist and photographer in addition to her position as best-selling novelist. Reprinted in *Backpacker* (August 16, 1976) under the title "Elder of the Tribe: Gene Stratton-Porter."

"Gene Stratton-Porter: The Fourth in Our Series of Pictorial American Romances." *Delineator* XCVI (May 1920), 24. Pictures of Porter at ten, sixteen, twenty, twenty-five, thirty, and fifty years of age with captions which sketch the life and career of the author.

HART, IRVING HARLOW. "The One Hundred Leading Authors of Best Sellers in Fiction from 1895 to 1944." *Publishers' Weekly* CXLIX (January 19, 1946), 285ff. Hart wrote frequently on the subject of popularity for *Publishers' Weekly;* for example, "The Most Popular Authors of Fiction between 1900 and 1925" (Feb. 21, 1925), and ". . . in the Post War Period 1919-1926" (Jan. 29, 1921). Porter, of course, is considered in all these articles.

HILL, HERBERT R. "Limberlost Author: Gene Stratton-Porter." *Outdoor Indiana* XXXIII (April 1968), 26-27, 38. A modern-day Hoosier writes breezily and somewhat inaccurately of Mrs. Porter, her life, and her writing and stresses her importance as a naturalist.

"Life and Writings." *Bookman* XLI (August 1915), 589-95. Another biographical sketch written midway of Porter's career and drawing on already published sources; interesting in that it gives a contemporary view of the author.

"Lover of the Great Out of Doors." *Ladies' Home Journal* XXXII (June 1915), 2. Almost identical comment can be made of this article as of the one immediately above.

McMULLEN, MARGARET. "Love's Old Sweetish Song." *Harper's Magazine* CXCV (October 1947), 371-80. A nostalgic look at the past; pokes gentle fun at the times and specifically at Gene Stratton Porter, Harold Bell Wright, and Florence Barclay.

MEEHAN, JEANNETTE PORTER. "My Mother." *McCall's Magazine* LII (January 1925), 18-19, 76. An account evidently written before Porter's death; of interest in that it recounts professional and social life of the author after her move to California—material not found in other sources.

"Mrs. Porter and Nature." *Bookman* XXXV (August 1912), 587-89. Still another contemporary biographical sketch, this one stresses the love and influence of nature apparent in her work.

PECKHAM, HOWARD R. "What Made Hoosiers Write?" *American Heritage* II (Autumn 1950), 58-62. Has material about the Western Association of Writers and Porter's involvement in it; also, general information about Porter.

SMITH, HARRISON. "Twenty Five Years of Best Sellers." *English Journal* XXXIII (October 1944), 401-408. Criticism from the academic viewpoint; dismisses as without value those who published prior to 1926 and became best-sellers, but promotes many who did not achieve this status.

5. Miscellany

BARRY, THOMAS J. "A Biographical and Bibliographical Dictionary of Indiana Authors." M.A. Thesis, University of Notre Dame, 1943. Useful checklist of Indiana writers and their output.

BEESON, R. KATHERINE. *Literary Indiana.* Pamphlet prepared as handout for NEA Convention of 1925. Indianapolis: Bobbs-Merrill, 1925, pp. 1–35. Short but useful account of the Indiana literary scene.

CLOTHIER, ANASTASIA. *Limberlost Cabin and Wildflower Woods.* Pamphlet, n.p., 1936, pp. 1–16. The story, written by the author's grandniece, of Mrs. Porter's building of Limberlost North and of the establishment of the nature preserve surrounding it—much intimate detail.

"Gene Stratton-Porter: Best Seller." Fort Wayne and Allen County Public Library, 1953, pp. 1–15. Porter from the librarian's point of view and expressing pride in the local girl made good. Has some interesting statistics on the circulation of Porter titles in this area of Indiana.

Gene Stratton Porter, Author and Naturalist. Booklet. Indianapolis: Indiana Department of Conservation, Division of Lands and Waters, August 1952 (reprinted November 1974) pp. 1–23. Booklet sold at the two memorial homes of Porter. Admittedly taken from the Meehan book with permission.

The Gene Stratton Porter State Memorial, Home of Gene Stratton Porter, and *The Limberlost State Memorial, Home of Gene Stratton Porter.* Indianapolis: Indiana Department of Conservation, 1947 (reprinted several times), pp. 1–4. These two leaflets used as advertising and as handouts at the memorials at Rome City and Geneva contain capsulated information about the author. Note that "Stratton Porter" not hyphenated.

Historical Booklet. Geneva Area Centennial, 1972, Inc., Geneva, Indiana: Historical Booklet Committee, 1972, pp. 1–64. Pages 42–49 of this booklet are devoted to Porter, and there are many references throughout to the author and to her husband, who were the town's leading citizens.

ROSE, GRACE D. "Limberlost Lady: A Story of Gene Stratton-Porter." TS. in Indiana State Library, 1968(?), pp. 1–53. In addition to the biographical sketch drawn from the usual sources, contains short synopses of the novels.

RUSSELL, NORENE A. "Gene Stratton-Porter, Nature Lover." TS. (mimeo) in Indiana State Library, 1963, pp. 1–12. A paper read before an unidentified meeting (but supposedly of "The Round Table," a literary society in Wabash, Indiana). Made up almost entirely of quotations from Porter but containing bits of information not found elsewhere.

SAMPLE, HAZEL. "Pitfalls for Readers of Fiction." Pamphlet Publication of the National Council of Teachers of English, No. 1. Chicago: NCTE, 1939–40, pp. 1–35. A comparative study of the work of Porter, Zane Grey, Harold Bell Wright, and Emilie Loring, claiming that each makes certain assumptions that the reader is supposed to accept, and that the unquestioning acceptance of these premises constitutes the "pitfalls" of reading.

WALLACE, FRANK NICOL. "Gene Stratton-Porter and Her Studies of Native Plants." TS. (mimeo) in Indiana State Library, 1925, pp. 2–5L. A paper read at the March 1925 meeting of the Garden Flowers Society of Fort Wayne, Indiana. Mr. Wallace was a longtime friend and associate of Gene Stratton Porter, having been the tree surgeon who worked at Wildflower Woods. Contains much intimate detail concerning the preservation of Indiana trees, shrubs, and flowers.

Index

The works of Porter are listed under her name